Criminal Justice & Immigration Act 2008

(under 18s)

Fergus Smith
B.Sc.(Hons), M.A., C.Q.S.W., D.M.S., Dip.M

Paul Carr
M.A.(Cantab), District Judge (Magistrates' Courts)

Children Act Enterprises Ltd
Pantiles Langham Road
Robertsbridge
East Sussex TN32 5EP
tel: 01580 880243

www.caeuk.org

© Fergus Smith 2009

British Library Cataloguing in Publication Data
A catalogue record for this book is available from the
British Library

ISBN 978-1-899986-14-9

Designed and typeset by Andrew Haig & Associates
Printed in the UK by The Lavenham Press

CAE is an independent organisation which publishes
guides to family and criminal law and provides
consultancy, research, training and independent
investigation services to the public, private and voluntary
sectors.

Contents

PART 4
Other Criminal Justice Provisions

PART 8
Anti-social Behaviour

Anti-social Behaviour

Appendices:

Abbreviations:

CA 1989 = Children Act 1989
CJA 2003 = Criminal Justice Act 2003
CDA 1998 = Crime and Disorder Act 1998

Introduction

- This guide offers a succinct and accurate summary of the provisions of the Criminal Justice and Immigration Act 2008 relevant to those aged less than 18 years old.

- Government had set out potential reforms to youth justice in 'Youth Justice – the next steps' published in 2003 as a companion to 'Every Child Matters' (www.everychildmatters.gov.uk). In 2004, responses to the above and government's consequent proposals were issued (www.homeoffice.gov.uk/documents/cons-youth-jus-next-steps-summ/). By 2007 a summary of responses to a further consultation paper 'Strengthening powers to tackle anti-social behaviour' was published (www.homeoffice.gov.uk/documents/cons-asb-powers/?version=1).

- The resulting Act received Royal Assent on 08.05.08. Part 1 (ss.1–8 and Schs.1–4) introduced 'Youth Rehabilitation Orders (YROs), a generic community sentence for children/young persons. This guide sets out the menu of requirements that may be attached and provisions for enforcement, revocation and amendment.

- Other provisions relevant to under 18 year olds are:

  - Clarification of the purposes of sentencing
  - Reviews of Anti-Social Behaviour Orders (ASBOs) etc
  - Amendments to Individual Support Orders (ISOs)

Definitions Relevant to Part 1 [s.7] [in alphabetical order]

Accommodation

- Except when the contrary intention appears, 'accommodation provided by or on behalf of a local authority' has the same meaning as it has in s.105 Children Act 1989 (see appendix 2 for CAE's guide to that Act).

Activity Requirement

- 'Activity requirement', in relation to a YRO has the meaning given by para. 6 of Sch.1 (see page 14).

Age Determination

- For the purposes of any provision of Part 1 which requires the determination of a person's age by the court, Secretary of State or local authority, it is that which it appears to the court/Secretary of State/ local authority to be, after considering any available evidence [s.7(2)].

Attendance Centre

- 'Attendance centre' has the meaning given by s.221(2) Criminal Justice Act 2003 and 'attendance centre requirement', in relation to a YRO has the meaning given by para. 12 of Sch.1 (see page 24).

Curfew Requirement

- 'Curfew requirement', in relation to a YRO has the meaning given by para.14 of Sch.1 (see page 27).

Custodial Sentence

- 'Custodial sentence' has the meaning given by s.76 Powers of Criminal Courts (Sentencing) Act 2000.

Detention & Training Order

- 'Detention and Training Order' has the same meaning as in s.163 Powers of Criminal Courts (Sentencing) Act 2000.

Drug Treatment Requirement

- 'Drug treatment requirement', in relation to a YRO has the meaning given by para.22 of Sch.1 (see page 40)

Drug Testing Requirement

- 'Drug testing requirement', in relation to a YRO has the meaning given by para.23 of Schedule 1 (see page 42).

Education Requirement

- 'Education requirement', in relation to a YRO has the meaning given by para.25 of Sch.1 (see page 46).

Electronic Monitoring Requirement

■ 'Electronic monitoring requirement", in relation to a YRO has the meaning given by para. 26 of Sch.1 (see page 48).

Exclusion Requirement

■ 'Exclusion requirement', in relation to a YRO has the meaning given by para. 15 of Schedule 1 (see page 28)

Extended Activity Requirement

■ 'Extended activity requirement', in relation to a YRO has the meaning given by para. 3 of Sch.1 (see page 70).

Fostering Requirement

■ 'Fostering requirement' in relation to a YRO with fostering, has the meaning given by para.18 of Sch.1 (see page 33).

Guardian

■ 'Guardian" has the same meaning as in the Children and Young Persons Act 1933.

Intoxicating Substance Treatment Requirement

■ 'Intoxicating substance treatment requirement', in relation to a YRO has the meaning given by para.24 of Sch.1 (see page 44)

Local Authority

- 'Local authority' means, in relation to:
  - England, a county council, a district council whose district does not form part of an area that has a county council, a London borough council, or the Common Council of the City of London in its capacity as a local authority, and
  - Wales, a county council, or a county borough council

Local Authority Residence Requirement

- 'Local authority residence requirement', in relation to a YRO has the meaning given by para.17 of Sch.1 (see page 31).

Local Probation Board

- 'Local probation board' means a local probation board established under s.4 Criminal Justice and Court Services Act 2000.

Mental Health Treatment Requirement

- 'Mental health treatment requirement' in relation to a YRO has the meaning given by para. 20 of Sch.1 (see page 36).

Programme Requirement

- 'Programme requirement', in relation to a YRO, has the meaning given by para.11 of Sch.1 (see page 22)

Prohibited Activity Requirement

■ 'Prohibited activity requirement', in relation to YRO has the meaning given by para.13 of Sch.1 (see page 26).

Qualifying Officer

■ In s.4 'qualifying officer', in relation to a YRO means:

  • A member of a youth offending team (YOT) established by a local authority for the time being specified in the order for the purposes of s.4, or
  • An officer of a local probation board appointed for or assigned to the local justice area for the time being so specified or (as the case may be) an officer of a provider of probation services acting in the local justice area [s.4(2)]

Residence Requirement

■ 'Residence requirement' in relation to a YRO has the meaning given by para. 16 of Sch.1 (see page 29).

Responsible Officer

■ For the purposes of Part 1, the 'the responsible officer' in relation to an offender to whom a YRO relates, means:

  • In a case when the order imposes a curfew requirement or an exclusion requirement but no other requirement mentioned in s.1(1), and

imposes an electronic monitoring requirement,
the person who under para.26(4) of Sch.1 is
responsible for the electronic monitoring required
by the order

- In a case when the only requirement imposed by
the order is an attendance centre requirement,
the officer in charge of the attendance centre in
question

- In any other case, the qualifying officer who, as
respects the offender, is for the time being
responsible for discharging the functions
conferred by Part 1 on the responsible officer
[s.4(1)]

Supervision Requirement

■ 'Supervision requirement' in relation to a YRO has the
meaning given by para.9 of Sch.1 (see page 19).

Unpaid Work Requirement

■ 'Unpaid work requirement', in relation to a YRO has
the meaning given by para. 10 of Sch.1 (see page
20).

Youth Offending Team

■ 'Youth offending team' (YOT) means a team
established under s.39 Crime and Disorder Act 1998.

Youth Rehabilitation Order

- 'Youth Rehabilitation Order' has the meaning given by s.1 (see page 10).

Youth Rehabilitation Order with Fostering

- 'Youth Rehabilitation Order with Fostering' has the meaning given by para.4 of Sch.1 (see page 70).

Youth Rehabilitation Order with Intensive Supervision & Surveillance

- 'Youth Rehabilitation Order with Intensive Supervision and Surveillance' has the meaning given by paragraph 3 of Sch.1 (see page 70).

YOUTH REHABILITATION ORDERS

Youth Rehabilitation Orders [Part 1 & Schs.1–4]

■ When a person aged less than 18 is convicted of an offence, the court by or before which s/he is convicted, may in accordance with Sch.1 make a 'Youth Rehabilitation Order' (YRO) imposing any one or more of the following requirements specified in s.1(1):

- An activity requirement (see paras. 6–8 Sch.1)
- A supervision requirement (see para. 9 Sch.1)
- In a case where the offender is aged 16 or 17 at the time of the conviction, an unpaid work requirement (see para.10 Sch. 1)
- A programme requirement (see para.11 Sch.1)
- An attendance centre requirement (see para.12 Sch.1)
- A prohibited activity requirement (see para.13 Sch.1)
- A curfew requirement (see para.14 Sch.1),
- An exclusion requirement (see para.15 Sch.1)
- A residence requirement (see para.16 Sch.1)
- A local authority residence requirement (see para.17 Sch.1)
- A mental health treatment requirement (see para.20 Sch.1)
- A drug treatment requirement (see para.22 Sch.1)
- A drug testing requirement (see para.23 Sch.1)

- An intoxicating substance treatment requirement (see para.24 Sch.1)
- An education requirement (see para.25 Sch.1) [s.1(1)]

■ A YRO:

- May also impose an electronic monitoring requirement (see para. 26 Sch.1), and
- Must do so if para.2 Sch. 1 so requires [s.1(2)]

■ A YRO may be with:

- Intensive supervision and surveillance (see para.3 Sch.1), or
- Fostering (see para. 4 Sch.1) [s.1(3)]

NB. Conditions which must be satisfied before imposition of a YRO with intensive supervision and surveillance or with fostering are outlined on page 70.

■ A court may only make an order mentioned in s.1(3) above if it is:

- Dealing with the offender for an offence which is punishable with imprisonment
- Of the opinion that the offence, or the combination of the offence and one or more offences associated with it, was so serious that, but for paras.3 or 4 of Sch.1 (YRO with intensive supervision and surveillance or with fostering), a custodial sentence would be appropriate (or, if the offender was aged under 12 at the time of

conviction, would be appropriate if the offender had been aged 12), and

- (If s/he was aged under 15 at the time of conviction), of the opinion the offender is a persistent offender [s.1(4)]

■ Sch. 1 makes further provision about YROs summarised immediately below and s.1 is subject to ss.148 and 150 Criminal Justice Act 2003 (restrictions on community sentences etc.), and provisions of Parts 1 and 3 of Sch.1 [s.1(5);(6)].

Requirements

Imposition of a YRO is subject to the following provisions each of which relate to particular requirements.

Activity Requirement [Sch.1 Para.6]

■ In this Part of the Act 'activity requirement', in relation to a YRO means a requirement that the offender must do any or all of the following:

- Participate, on such number of days as may be specified in the order in activities at a place, or places, so specified
- Participate in an activity, or activities, specified in the order on such number of days as may be so specified
- Participate in one or more residential exercises for a continuous period or periods comprising such number or numbers of days as may be specified in the order
- In accordance with para.7 below, engage in activities in accordance with instructions of the responsible officer on such number of days as may be specified in the order [Sch.1 para.6(1)]

■ Subject to para.3(2), the number of days specified in the order under para.6(1) must not, in aggregate, be more than 90 [Sch.1 para.6(2)].

■ A requirement such as mentioned in the 1st 2 round bullet points of para. 6(1) above, operates to require the offender, in accordance with instructions given by the responsible officer, on the number of days specified in the order in relation to the requirement:

- In the case of a requirement such as mentioned in the 1st round bullet point of para.6(1), to present her/himself at a place specified in the order to a person of a description so specified, or

- In the case of a requirement such as mentioned in the 2nd round bullet point, to participate in an activity specified in the order

■ On each such day as specified above, the offender must comply with instructions given by, or under the authority of, the person in charge of the place or the activity (as the case may be) [Sch.1 para.6(3)]

■ If the order requires the offender to participate in a residential exercise, it must specify:

- A place, or
- An activity [Sch.1 para.6(4)]

■ A requirement to participate in a residential exercise operates to require the offender, in accordance with instructions given by the responsible officer:

- If a place is specified under para. 6(4), to present her/himself at the beginning of the period specified, at the place so specified to a person of a description specified in the instructions, and reside there for that period
- If an activity is specified under para. 6(4) to participate, for the period specified in the activity so specified

■ During the relevant period, the offender must comply with instructions given by, or under the authority of the person in charge of the place or activity [Sch.1 para. 6(5)].

Activity Requirement: Instructions of Responsible Officer & Further Provisions [Sch.1 para.7]

- Subject to para. 7(3), instructions under the fourth option of Sch.1 para.6(1) relating to any day must require the offender to do either of the following:

  - Present him/herself to a person/s of a description specified in the instructions at a place so specified
  - Participate in an activity specified in the instructions [Sch.1 para. 7(1)]

- Any such instructions operate to require the offender, on that day or while participating in that activity, to comply with instructions given by, or under the authority of, the person in charge of the place or, as the case may be, the activity [Sch.1 para.7(2)].

- If the order so provides, instructions under the final roundel of para.6(1) may require the offender to participate in a residential exercise for a period of not more than 7 days, and, for that purpose, to:

  - Present her/himself at the beginning of that period to a person of a description specified in the instructions at a place so specified and to reside there for that period, or
  - Participate for that period in an activity specified in the instructions [Sch.1 para.7(3)]

- The instructions in para 7(3) above:

  - May not be given except with the consent of a parent or guardian of the offender, and

- Operate to require the offender, during the period specified, to comply with instructions given by, or under the authority of, the person in charge of place/activity specified in sub-para.3 [Sch.1 para.7(4)]

  NB. Instructions given by, or under the authority of, a person in charge of any place under the following provisions may require the offender to engage in activities otherwise than at that place – para.6(3),para.6(5), para.7(2), or para.7(4)(b) [Sch.1 para.8]

■ An activity specified in an order under the second round bullet point of para.6(1) or in instructions given under the fourth one, may consist of or include an activity whose purpose is that of reparation, e.g. an activity involving contact between an offender and persons affected by the offences in respect of which the order was made [Sch.1 para.8(2)].

■ A court may not include an activity requirement in a YRO unless it:

  - Has consulted a member of a YOT, an officer of a local probation board or an officer of a provider of probation services
  - Is satisfied that it is feasible to secure compliance with the requirement, and
  - Is satisfied provision for the offender to participate in the activities proposed to be specified in the order can be made under the arrangements for persons to participate in such

activities which exist in the local justice area in which the offender resides or is to reside [Sch.1 para.8(3)]

■ A court may not include an activity requirement in a YRO if compliance with that requirement would involve the co-operation of a person other than the offender and the responsible officer, unless that other person consents to its inclusion [Sch.1 para.8(4)].

Supervision Requirement [Sch.1 Para.9]

■ In this Part of the Act 'supervision requirement', in relation to a YRO, means a requirement that, during the period for which the order remains in force, the offender must attend appointments with the responsible officer or another person determined by the responsible officer, at such times and places as may be determined by the responsible officer [Sch.1 para.9].

Unpaid Work Requirement [Sch.1 Para.10]

■ In Part 1 of the Act 'unpaid work requirement', in relation to a YRO means a requirement that the offender must perform unpaid work in accordance with para.10 [Sch.1 para. 10(1)].

■ The number of hours which a person may be required to work under an unpaid work requirement must be specified in the YRO and must be, in aggregate:

• Not less than 40, and
• Not more than 240 [Sch.1 para.10(2)]

■ A court may not impose an unpaid work requirement in respect of an offender unless:

• After hearing (if the court thinks necessary) an 'appropriate officer', the court is satisfied that the offender is a suitable person to perform work under such a requirement, and
• The court is satisfied that provision for the offender to work under such a requirement can be made under the arrangements for persons to perform work under such a requirement which exist in the local justice area in which the offender resides or is to reside [Sch.1 para.10(3)]

NB. An 'appropriate officer' here means a member of a YOT, officer of a local probation board or an officer of a provider of probation services [Sch.1 para.10(4)].

- An offender in respect of whom an unpaid work requirement of a YRO is in force must perform for the number of hours specified in the order, such work at such times as the responsible officer may specify in instructions [Sch.1 para.10(5)].

- Subject to Sch.2 para. 17 (extension of unpaid work requirement see p. 110) , the work required to be performed under an unpaid work requirement of a YRO must be performed during the period of 12 months beginning with the day on which the order takes effect [Sch.1 para.10(6)].

- Unless revoked, a YRO imposing an unpaid work requirement remains in force until the offender has worked under it for the number of hours specified in it [Sch.1 para.10(7)].

Programme Requirement [Sch.1 Para.11]

■ In this Part of the Act 'programme requirement', in relation to a YRO means a requirement that the offender must participate in a systematic set of activities ('a programme') specified in the order at a place or places so specified on such number of days as may be so specified [Sch.1 para.11(1)].

■ A programme requirement may require the offender to reside at any place specified in the order under para. 11(1) for any period so specified if it is necessary for the offender to reside there for that period in order to participate in the programme [Sch.1 para.11(2)].

■ A court may not include a programme requirement in a youth rehabilitation order unless:

  • The programme which the court proposes to specify in the order has been recommended to the court by a member of a YOT, officer of a local probation board, or an officer of a provider of probation services, as being suitable for the offender, and
  • The court is satisfied that the programme is available at the place or places proposed to be specified [Sch.1 para.11(3)]

■ A court may not include a programme requirement in a YRO if compliance with that requirement would involve the co-operation of a person other than the offender and the offender's responsible officer, unless that other person consents to its inclusion [Sch.1 para.11(4)].

■ A requirement to participate in a programme operates to require the offender:

- In accordance with instructions given by the responsible officer to participate in the programme at the place or places specified in the order on the number of days so specified, and
- While at any of those places, to comply with instructions given by, or under the authority of, the person in charge of the programme [Sch.1 para.11(5)]

Attendance Centre Requirement [Sch.1 Para.12]

■ In Part 1 of the Act 'attendance centre requirement', in relation to a YRO means a requirement the offender must attend a specified attendance centre for the hours specified [Sch.1 para.12(1)].

■ The aggregate number of hours for attendance:

• If the offender is aged 16 or over at the time of conviction, must be not less than 12, and not more than 36
• If the offender is aged 14 or over but under 16 at the time of conviction, must be not less than 12, and not more than 24
• If the offender is aged under 14 at the time of conviction, must not be more than 12 [Sch.1 para.12(2)]

■ A court may not include an attendance centre requirement in a YRO unless it:

• Has been notified by the Secretary of State that an attendance centre is available for persons of the offender's description, and provision can be made at the centre for the offender, and
• Is satisfied that the attendance centre proposed to be specified is reasonably accessible to the offender, having regard to the means of access available to the offender and any other circumstances [Sch.1 para.12(3)]

- The first time at which the offender is required to attend at the attendance centre is a time notified to the offender by the responsible officer [Sch.1 para.12(4)].

- The subsequent hours are to be fixed by the officer in charge of the centre:

    - In accordance with arrangements made by the responsible officer and
    - Having regard to the offender's circumstances [Sch.1 para.(5)]

- An offender may not be required under para.12 to attend at an attendance centre:

    - On more than 1 occasion on any day, or
    - For more than 3 hours on any occasion [Sch.1 para.12(6)]

- A requirement to attend at an attendance centre for any period on any occasion operates as a requirement:

    - To attend at the centre at the beginning of the period, and
    - During that period, to engage in occupation, or receive instruction, under the supervision of and in accordance with instructions given by, or under the authority of, the officer in charge of the centre, at the centre or elsewhere [Sch.1 para.12(7)]

Prohibited Activity Requirement [Sch.1 Para.13]

■ In this Part of the Act 'prohibited activity requirement' in relation to a YRO means a requirement that the offender must refrain from participating in activities specified in the order:

- On a day or days so specified, or
- During a period so specified [Sch.1 para.13(1)]

■ A court may not include a prohibited activity requirement in a YRO unless it has consulted:

- A member of a YOT
- An officer of a local probation board, or
- An officer of a provider of probation services [Sch.1 para.13(2)]

■ The requirements that may by virtue of para.13 be included in a YRO include a requirement that the offender does not possess, use or carry a firearm within the meaning of the Firearms Act 1968 [Sch.1 para.13(3)].

Curfew Requirement [Sch.1 Para.14]

- In this Part of the Act 'curfew requirement', in relation to a YRO means a requirement that the offender must remain, for periods specified in the order, at a place so specified [Sch.1 para.14(1)].

- A YRO imposing a curfew requirement may specify different places or different periods for different days, but may not specify periods which amount to less than 2 hours or more than 12 hours in any day [Sch.1 para.14(2)].

- A YRO imposing a curfew requirement may not specify periods which fall outside the period of 6 months beginning with the day on which the requirement first takes effect [Sch.1 para. 14(3)].

- Before making a YRO imposing a curfew requirement, the court must obtain and consider information about the place proposed to be specified in the order including information as to the attitude of persons likely to be affected by the enforced presence there of the offender) [Sch.1 para.14(4)].

Exclusion Requirement [Sch.1 Para.15]

■ In this Part of the Act 'exclusion requirement', in relation to a YRO means a provision prohibiting the offender from entering a place (includes area) specified in the order for a period so specified [Sch.1 para. 15(1);(4)].

■ The period specified must not be more than 3 months [Sch.1 para. 15(2)].

■ An exclusion requirement:

  • May provide for the prohibition to operate only during the periods specified in the order, and
  • May specify different places for different periods or days [Sch.1 para. 15(3)]

Residence Requirement [Sch.1 Para.16]

- In this Part of the Act, 'residence requirement', in relation to a YRO means a requirement that, during the period specified in the order, the offender must reside:

  - With an individual specified in the order, or
  - At a place specified in the order (a 'place of residence requirement') [Sch.1 para.16(1);(3)]

- A court may not by virtue of the first of the above requirements include a requirement that the offender reside with an individual unless that individual has consented to the requirement [Sch.1 para.16(2)].

- A court may not include a 'place of residence requirement' in a YRO unless the offender was aged 16 or over at the time of conviction [Sch.1 para.16(4)].

- If the order so provides, a 'place of residence requirement' does not prohibit the offender from residing, with the prior approval of the responsible officer, at a place other than that specified in the order [Sch.1 para.16(5)].

- Before making a YRO containing a 'place of residence requirement', the court must consider the home surroundings of the offender [Sch.1 para.16(6)].

■ A court may not specify a hostel or other institution as the place where an offender must reside for the purposes of a 'place of residence requirement' except on the recommendation of:

- A member of a YOT
- An officer of a local probation board,
- An officer of a provider of probation services, or
- A social worker of a local authority [Sch.1 para.16(7)]

Local Authority Residence Requirement [Sch.1 Para.17]

■ In this Part of the Act, 'local authority residence requirement', in relation to a YRO means a requirement that, during the period specified in the order, the offender must reside in accommodation provided by or on behalf of a local authority specified in the order for the purposes of the requirement [Sch.1 para.17(1)].

■ A YRO which imposes a 'local authority residence requirement' may also stipulate that the offender is not to reside with a person specified in the order [Sch.1 para.17(2)].

■ A court may not include a 'local authority residence requirement' in a YRO made in respect of an offence unless it is satisfied that the:

  • Behaviour which constituted the offence was due to a significant extent to the circumstances in which the offender was living, and
  • Imposition of that requirement will assist in the offender's rehabilitation [Sch.1 para.17(3)]

■ A court may not include a 'local authority residence requirement' in a YRO unless it has consulted:

  • A parent or guardian of the offender (unless it is impracticable to consult her/him), and
  • The local authority which is to receive the offender [Sch.1 para.17(4)]

■ A YRO which imposes a 'local authority residence requirement' must specify, as the authority which is to receive the offender, the local authority in whose area the offender resides or is to reside [Sch.1 para.17(5)].

■ Any period specified in a YRO as a period for which the offender must reside in accommodation provided by or on behalf of a local authority must not:

   • Be longer than 6 months, and
   • Include any period after the offender has reached the age of 18 [Sch.1 para.17(6)]

Fostering Requirement [Sch.1 Para.18]

■ In this Part of the Act 'fostering requirement', in relation to a YRO means a requirement that, for a period specified in the order, the offender must reside with a local authority foster parent [Sch.1 para.18(1)].

■ A period specified in a YRO for which the offender must reside with a local authority foster parent must:

- End no later than the end of the period of 12 months beginning with the date on which the requirement first has effect (but subject to paras. 6(9), 8(9) and 16(2) of Sch. 2 which set out respective courts' powers in specified circumstances to substitute new fostering requirement and extend the maximum period form the YRO was first made), and
- Not include any period after the offender has reached the age of 18 [Sch.1 para.18(2)]

■ A YRO which imposes a fostering requirement must specify the local authority which is to place the offender with a local authority foster parent under s.23(2)(a) Children Act 1989 [Sch.1 para. 18(3)].

■ The authority so specified must be the local authority in whose area the offender resides or is to reside [Sch.1 para. 18(4)].

■ The fostering requirement is, until the determination of the application, to be taken to require the offender to reside in accommodation provided by or on behalf of a local authority, if at any time during the period specified under para. 18(1), the responsible officer notifies the offender that:

- No suitable local authority foster parent is available, and
- The responsible officer has applied or proposes to apply under Part 3 or 4 of Sch.2 for the revocation or amendment of the order [Sch.1 para. 18(5)]

■ Para.18 does not affect the power of a local authority to place with a local authority foster parent an offender in respect of whom a local authority residence requirement is imposed [Sch.1 para. 18(6)].

■ A court may not include a fostering requirement in a YRO unless the court has been notified by the Secretary of State that arrangements for implementing such a requirement are available in the area of the local authority which is to place the offender with a local authority foster parent [Sch.1 para. 18(7)].

NB. In para.18 'local authority foster parent' means the same as in the Children Act 1989 [Sch.1 para.18(8)].

**Pre-conditions to Imposing Local Authority
Residence Requirements or Fostering Requirement
[Sch.1 Para.19]**

■ A court may not include a local authority residence
requirement or a fostering requirement in a YRO in
respect of an offender unless:

   • The offender was legally represented at the
     relevant time in court, or
   • Either of the conditions in para.19(2) below is
     satisfied [Sch.1 para. 19(1)]

■ Those conditions are that the offender:

   • Was granted a right to representation funded by
     the Legal Services Commission as part of the
     Criminal Defence Service for the purposes of the
     proceedings but the right was withdrawn
     because of the offender's conduct, or
   • Has been informed of the right to apply for such
     representation for purposes of the proceedings,
     has had the opportunity to do so, but
     nevertheless refused or failed to apply [Sch.1
     para. 19(2)]

*NB. In para.19 'the proceedings' means the whole
proceedings, or the part of them relating to
imposition of the local authority residence/fostering
requirement; 'relevant time' means the time the court
is considering whether to impose that requirement
[Sch.1 para.19(3)].*

Mental Health Treatment Requirement [Sch.1 Para.20]

■ In this Part 'mental health treatment requirement', in relation to YRO means a requirement the offender must submit, during a period/s specified in the order, to treatment by/under the direction of a registered medical practitioner or chartered psychologist (or both, for different periods) with a view to the improvement of the offender's mental condition [Sch.1 para. 20(1)].

■ Though the order must not otherwise specify the nature of the treatment required during a period specified under para.20(1), it must be such one of the following as may be specified in the YRO:

• Treatment as a resident patient in an independent hospital or care home within the meaning of the Care Standards Act 2000 or a hospital within the meaning of the Mental Health Act 1983 but not in hospital premises where high security psychiatric services within the meaning of that Act are provided

• Treatment as a non-resident patient at such institution or place as may be specified in the order

• Treatment by or under the direction of such registered medical practitioner or chartered psychologist (or both) as may be so specified [Sch.1 para.20(2)]

■ A court may not include a mental health treatment requirement in a YRO unless:

- The court is satisfied, on the evidence of a registered medical practitioner approved for purposes of s.12 Mental Health Act 1983 that the mental condition of the offender is such as requires and may be susceptible to treatment, but is not such as to warrant making a hospital order or guardianship order under that Act,
- The court is also satisfied that arrangements have been or can be made for the treatment intended to be specified in the order incl. if the offender is to be required to submit to treatment as a resident patient, arrangements for her/his reception and
- The offender has expressed willingness to comply with the requirement [Sch.1 para.20(3)]

■ While the offender is under treatment as a resident patient in pursuance of a mental health treatment requirement of a YRO, the responsible officer is to carry out the supervision of the offender to such extent only as may be necessary for the purpose of revocation or amendment of the order [Sch.1 para.20(4)].

■ S.54(2);(3) Mental Health Act 1983 have effect with respect to proof of an offender's mental condition for purposes of the first condition of para. 20(3) above as they have effect with respect to proof of an offender's mental condition for purposes of s.37(2)(a) of that Act [Sch.1 para. 20(5)].

*NB. In paras. 20 and 21, 'chartered psychologist'
means a person for the time being listed in the British
Psychological Society's Register of Chartered
Psychologists [Sch.1 para.20(6)].*

Mental Health Treatment at Place Other Than Specified in Order [Sch.1 Para.21]

■ Either may make arrangements for the offender to be treated accordingly if the registered medical practitioner or chartered psychologist by whom, or under whose direction an offender is being treated in pursuance of a mental health treatment requirement is of the opinion that part of the treatment can be better or more conveniently given in or at an institution or place which:

- Is not specified in the YRO, and
- Is one in, or at which the treatment of the offender will be given by or under the direction of a registered medical practitioner or chartered psychologist [Sch.1 para.21(1)]

■ Such arrangements may only be made if the offender has expressed willingness for the treatment to be given as mentioned in para. 21(1) [Sch.1 para.21(2)].

■ Such arrangements as are mentioned in para. 21(1) may provide for part of the treatment to be provided to the offender as a resident patient in an institution or place notwithstanding that the institution or place is not one which could have been specified for that purpose in the youth rehabilitation order [Sch.1 para.21(3)].

■ When any such arrangements as are mentioned in para. 21(1) are made for the treatment of an offender:

- The registered medical practitioner or chartered psychologist by whom the arrangements are made must give notice in writing to the offender's responsible officer, specifying the institution or place in/at which the treatment is to be carried out, and
- The treatment provided for by the arrangements is deemed to be treatment to which the offender is required to submit in pursuance of the YRO [Sch.1 para.21(4)]

Drug Treatment Requirement [Sch.1 Para.22]

■ In this Part of the Act, 'drug treatment requirement', in relation to a YRO means a requirement that the offender must submit, during a period/s specified in the order, to treatment, by or under the direction of a person so specified having the necessary qualifications or experience ('the treatment provider'), with a view to the reduction or elimination of the offender's dependency on, or propensity to misuse, drugs [Sch.1 para.22(1)]

■ A court may not include a drug treatment requirement in a YRO unless it is satisfied that:

- The offender is dependent on, or has a propensity to misuse, drugs, and that
- Her/his dependency or propensity is such as requires and may be susceptible to treatment [Sch.1 para.22(2)]

■ Though the order must not otherwise specify its nature the treatment required during a period specified under para.22(1) must be such one of the following kinds as may be specified in the YRO:

- Treatment as a resident in such institution or place as may be specified in the order, or
- Treatment as a non-resident at such institution or place, and at such intervals, as may be so specified [Sch.1 para.22(3)]

■ A court may not include a drug treatment requirement in a YRO unless:

- The court has been notified by the Secretary of State that arrangements for implementing drug treatment requirements are in force in the local justice area in which the offender resides/is to reside
- The court is satisfied that arrangements have been or can be made for the treatment intended to be specified in the order (including, if the offender is to be required to submit to treatment as a resident, arrangements for the reception of the offender),
- The requirement has been recommended to the court as suitable for the offender by a member of a YOT, an officer of a local probation board or an officer of a provider of probation services, and
- The offender has expressed willingness to comply with the requirement [Sch.1 para.22(4)]

NB. In para. 22 'drug' means a controlled drug as defined by s.2 Misuse of Drugs Act 1971 [Sch.1 para.22(5)].

Drug Testing Requirement [Sch.1 Para.23]

■ In this Part of the Act, 'drug testing requirement', in relation to a YRO, means a requirement that, for the purpose of ascertaining whether there is any drug in the offender's body during any treatment period, the offender must, during that period, provide samples in accordance with instructions given by the responsible officer or treatment provider [Sch.1 para.23(1)].

NB. In para. 23(1) 'drug' has the same meaning as in para.22; 'treatment period' means a period specified in the YRO as a period during which the offender must submit to treatment as mentioned in para.22(1) and 'treatment provider' has the meaning given by para.22 [Sch.1 para.23(2)].

■ A court may not include a drug testing requirement in a YRO unless the:

- Court has been notified by the Secretary of State that arrangements for implementing drug testing requirements are in force in the local justice area in which the offender resides or is to reside and
- Order also imposes a drug treatment requirement, and the
- Offender has expressed willingness to comply with the requirement [Sch.1 para.23(3)]

■ A YRO which imposes a drug testing requirement:

- • Must specify for each month the minimum number of occasions on which samples are to be provided, and
- • May specify times and circumstances in which the responsible officer/treatment provider may require samples to be provided, and descriptions of the samples which may be so required [Sch.1 para.23(4)]

■ A YRO which imposes a drug testing requirement must provide for the results of tests carried out otherwise than by the responsible officer on samples provided by the offender in pursuance of the requirement to be communicated to the responsible officer [Sch.1 para.23(5)].

Intoxicating Substance Misuse Treatment Requirement [Sch.1 Para.24]

■ In this Part of the Act, 'intoxicating substance treatment requirement', in relation to a YRO means a requirement that the offender must submit, during a period/s specified in the order, to treatment, by or under the direction of a person so specified having the necessary qualifications or experience, with a view to the reduction or elimination of the offender's dependency on or propensity to misuse intoxicating substances [Sch.1 para.23(1)].

■ A court may not include an intoxicating substance treatment requirement in a YRO unless it is satisfied that the:

- Offender is dependent on, or has a propensity to misuse, intoxicating substances, and
- Offender's dependency or propensity is such as requires and may be susceptible to treatment [Sch.1 para.24(2)]

■ Though the order must not otherwise specify its nature the treatment required during a period specified under para.24 (1) must be such one of the following kinds as may be specified in the YRO:

- Treatment as a resident in such institution or place as may be specified in the order, or

- Treatment as a non-resident at such institution or place, and at such intervals, as may be so specified [Sch.1 para.24(3)]

■ A court may not include an intoxicating substance treatment requirement in a YRO unless the:

- Court is satisfied that arrangements have been or can be made for the treatment intended to be specified in the order (incl. when the offender is to be required to submit to treatment as a resident, arrangements for her/his reception)
- Requirement has been recommended to the court as suitable for the offender by a member of a YOT, an officer of a local probation board or an officer of a provider of probation services, and
- Offender has expressed willingness to comply with the requirement [Sch.1 para.24(4)]

NB. In para.24 'intoxicating substance' means alcohol, or any other substance or product (other than a drug) which is, or the fumes of which are, capable of being inhaled or otherwise used for the purpose of causing intoxication and in para.24(5) 'drug' means a controlled drug as defined by s.2 Misuse of Drugs Act 1971[Sch. 1 para.24(5);(6)].

Education Requirement [Sch.1 Para.25]

■ In this Part of the Act 'education requirement' means a requirement the offender must comply, during a period/s specified in the order, with approved education arrangements [Sch.1 para.25(1)].

■ For this purpose, 'approved education arrangements' means arrangements for the offender's education:

   • Made for the time being by the offender's parent or guardian, and
   • Approved by the LEA specified in the order [Sch.1 para.25(2)]

■ The LEA so specified must be the authority for the area in which the offender resides or is to reside [Sch.1 para.25(3)].

■ A court may not include an education requirement in a YRO unless it has consulted the LEA proposed to be specified in the order with regard to the proposal to include the requirement, and it is satisfied that:

   • In the view of that LEA, arrangements exist for the offender to receive efficient full time education suitable to her/his age, ability, aptitude and special educational needs (if any), and
   • Having regard to the circumstances of the case, the inclusion of the education requirement is necessary for securing the good conduct of the

offender or for preventing commission of further offences [Sch.1 para.25(4)]

■ Any period specified in a YRO as a period during which an offender must comply with approved education arrangements must not include any period after s/he has ceased to be of compulsory school age [Sch.1 para.25(5)].

NB. In para.25, 'LEA' and 'parent' have the same meanings as in the Education Act 1996. [Sch.1 para.25(6)].

Electronic Monitoring Requirement [Sch.1 Para.26]

■ In this Part of the Act 'electronic monitoring requirement' means a requirement for securing the electronic monitoring of the offender's compliance with other requirements imposed by the order during a period specified in the order or determined by the responsible officer in accordance with the order [Sch.1 para.26(1)].

■ When an electronic monitoring requirement is required to take effect during a period determined by the responsible officer in accordance with the YRO, the responsible officer must, before the beginning of that period, notify its time to the:

- Offender
- Person responsible for the monitoring, and
- Any person specified in para.26(3) below [Sch.26(2)]

■ When it is proposed to include an electronic monitoring requirement in a YRO, but there is a person (other than the offender) without whose cooperation it will not be practicable to secure that the monitoring takes place, the requirement may not be included in the order without that person's consent [Sch.1 para.26(3)].

■ A YRO which imposes an electronic monitoring requirement must include provision for making a

Proposed requirements of YRO	Relevant Place
Curfew requirement	Place to which court proposes to specify in the order for the purposes of that requirement
Exclusion requirement	The place (within meaning of para.15) the court proposes to specify in the order
Attendance centre order	The attendance centre the court proposes to specify in the order

Power to Amend Limits [Sch.1 Para.27]

■ By substituting, for the maximum number of hours for the time being specified in that provision, such other number of hours as may be specified, the Secretary of State may by order amend:

- Para. 10(2) (unpaid work requirement), or
- Para. 14(2) (curfew requirement) [Sch.1 para. 27(1)]

■ The Secretary of State may by order amend any of the provisions mentioned in para.27 (3) below, by substituting, for any period for the time being specified in the provision, such other period as may be specified in the order [Sch.1 para.27(2)].

■ Those provisions are, in Sch.1:

- Para. 14(3) (curfew requirement)
- Para. 15(2) (exclusion requirement)
- Para. 17(6) (local authority residence requirement)
- Para. 18(2) (fostering requirement) [Sch.1 para.27(3)]

■ An order under para.27 which amends para.18(2) may also make consequential amendments of paras.6(9), 8(9) and 16(2) of Schedule 2 [Sch.1 para.27(4)] (see page 33).

Provisions Applying When Court Proposes to Make YRO (Sch. 1 Part 3)

Family Circumstances

- Before making a YRO, the court must obtain and consider information about the offender's family circumstances and the likely effect of such an order on those circumstances [Sch.1 para.28].

Compatibility of Requirements, Requirement to Avoid Conflict with Religious Beliefs, etc [Sch.1 Para.29]

■ Before making either a YRO imposing 2 or more requirements, or 2 or more YROs in respect of associated offences, the court must consider whether, in the circumstances of the case, the requirements to be imposed by the order/s are compatible with each other [Sch.1 para. 29(1)].

■ The above para.29 (1) is subject to paras.2 (electronic monitoring), 3(4) (mandatory requirements additional to an extended activity requirement) and 4(4) (fostering and supervision requirement) [Sch.1 para.29(2)]

■ The court must ensure, as far as practicable, that any requirement imposed by a YRO avoids any:

  • Conflict with the offender's religious beliefs
  • Interference with the times, if any, at which the offender normally works or attends school or any other educational establishment, and any
  • Conflict with the requirements of any other YRO to which the offender may be subject [Sch.1 para.29(3)]

■ The Secretary of State may by order provide that para.29(3) has effect with any additional restrictions specified in the order [Sch.1 para.29(4)]

Date of Taking Effect & Other Existing Orders [Sch.1 Para.30]

■ Subject to para.30(2), a YRO takes effect on the day after the day on which the order is made [Sch.1 para.30(1)].

■ If a detention and training order (DTO) is in force in respect of an offender, a court making a YRO may order that it is to take effect instead:

• When the period of supervision begins in relation to the DTO in accordance with s.103(1)(a) Powers of Criminal Courts (Sentencing) Act 2000 or

• On the expiry of the term of the DTO [Sch.1 para.30(2)]

NB. The above references to a DTO include an order made under s.211 Armed Forces Act 2006 (detention and training orders made by service courts) and the reference to s.103(1)(a) Powers of Criminal Courts (Sentencing) Act 2000 includes that provision as applied by s. 213(1) Armed Forces Act 2006 [Sch.1 para.30(3)].

■ A court must not make a YRO in respect of an offender at a time when another YRO or a Reparation Order made under s.73(1) Powers of Criminal Courts (Sentencing) Act 2000 is in force in respect of the offender, unless when it makes the order it revokes the earlier one [Sch.1 para. 30(4)]

- If the earlier order is revoked under para.30(4), para.24 of Schedule 2 (provision of copies of orders) applies to the revocation as it applies to the revocation of a YRO [Sch.1 para 30(50).

Concurrent & Consecutive Orders [Sch.1 Para.31]

- Para 30. applies when the court is dealing with an offender who has been convicted of 2 or more associated offences [Sch.1 para.31(1)].

- If, in respect of 1 of the offences, the court makes a YRO with intensive supervision and surveillance, a YRO with fostering, or any other YRO, it may not make an order of any other of those kinds in respect of the other offence, or any of the other offences [Sch.1 para.31(2)]

- If the court makes 2 or more YROs with intensive supervision and surveillance, or with fostering, both or all of the orders must take effect at the same time (in accordance with para.30(1) or (2)) [Sch.1 para. 31(3)].

- If the court includes requirements of the same kind in 2 or more YROs it must direct, in relation to each requirement of that kind, whether:

  - It is to be concurrent with the other requirement/s of that kind, or any of them, or
  - It and the other requirement or requirements of that kind, or any of them, are to be consecutive [Sch.1 para. 31(4)]

- The court may not direct that 2 or more fostering requirements are to be consecutive [Sch. 1 para. 31(5)].

■ If the court directs that 2 or more requirements of the same kind are to be consecutive:

- The number of hours, days or months specified in relation to one of them is additional to the number of hours, days, or months specified in relation to the other or others, but
- The aggregate number of hours, days or months specified in relation to both or all of them must not exceed the maximum number which may be specified in relation to any one of them [Sch.1 para.31(6)]

NB. For the purposes of paras. 31 (4) and (6), requirements are of the same kind if they fall within the same paragraph of Part 2 of this Schedule [Sch.1 para.31(7)].

Provisions Applying Where Court Makes YRO etc (Sch. 1 Part 4)

Date for Compliance with Requirements to be Specified in Order [Sch.1 Para.32]

- A YRO must specify a date, not more than 3 years after the date on which it takes effect, by which all the requirements in it must have been complied with [Sch.1 para. 32(1)].

- A YRO which imposes 2 or more different requirements falling within Part 2 of Schedule 1 may also specify an earlier date/in relation to compliance with any 1 or more of them [Sch.1 para.32(2)].

- In the case of a YRO with intensive supervision and surveillance, the date specified for the purposes of para.32(1) above must not be earlier than 6 months after the date on which the order takes effect [Sch.1 para.32(3)].

Local Justice Area to be Specified in Order [Sch.1 Para.33]

■ A YRO must specify the local justice area in which the offender resides or will reside [Sch.1 para.33].

Provision of Copies of Orders [Sch.1 Para.34]

■ The court by which any YRO is made must forthwith provide copies of the order:

- To the offender
- If the offender is aged under 14, to the offender's parent or guardian, and
- To a member of a YOT assigned to the court, to an officer of a local probation board assigned to the court or to an officer of a provider of probation services [Sch.1 para.34(1)]

■ When a YRO is made by the Crown Court, or a magistrates' court which does not act in the local justice area specified in the order, the court must:

- Provide to the magistrates' court acting in the local justice area specified in the order a copy of the order, and such documents and information relating to the case as it considers likely to be of assistance to a court acting in that area in the exercise of its functions in relation to the order and
- Provide a copy of the order to the local probation board acting for that area or (as the case may be) a provider of probation services operating in that area [Sch.1 para.34(2);(3)]

■ When a YRO imposes any requirement specified in the first column of the following table, the court by which the order is made must also forthwith provide the person specified in relation to that requirement in the second column with a copy of so much of the order as relates to that requirement.

Requirement	Person to whom copy of requirement to be given
An activity requirement specifying a place under para. 6(1)(a)	The person in charge of that place
An activity requirement specifying an activity under para. 6(1)(b)	The person in charge of that activity
An activity requirement specifying a residential exercise under para.6(1)(c)	The person in charge of the place or activity specified under para.6(4) in relation to that residential exercise
An attendance centre requirement	The officer in charge of the attendance centre specified under para.12(1)
An exclusion requirement imposed for the purpose (or partly for the purpose) of protecting a person from being approached by the offender	The person intended to be protected

Requirement	Person to whom copy of requirement to be given
A residence requirement requiring residence with an individual	The individual specified under para. 16(1)(a).
A place of residence requirement (within the meaning of para. 16) relating to residence in an institution	The person in charge of the institution
A local authority residence requirement	The local authority specified under para.17(1).
A mental health treatment requirement	The person in charge of the institution or place specified under para.20(2)(a) or (b) or the person specified under para.20(2)(c)
A drug treatment requirement	The treatment provider specified under para.22(1)
A drug testing requirement	The treatment provider specified under para.22(1).
An intoxicating substance treatment requirement	The person specified under para.24(1)
An education requirement	The local education authority specified under para.25(2)

Requirement	*Person to whom copy of requirement to be given*
An electronic monitoring requirement	Any person who by virtue of para.26(4) will be responsible for the electronic monitoring or any person without whose consent the requirement could not have been included in the order

Power to Provide for Court Review of Orders [Sch.1 Para.35]

■ The Secretary of State may by order:

- Enable or require a court making a YRO to provide for the order to be reviewed periodically by that or another court,
- Enable a court to amend a YRO so as to include or remove a provision for review by a court, and
- Make provision as to the timing and conduct of reviews and as to the powers of the court on a review [Sch.1 para.35(1)]

■ An order under paragraph 35 may, in particular, make provision in relation to YROs corresponding to any provision made by s.191 and s.192 Criminal Justice Act 2003 (reviews of suspended sentence orders) in relation to suspended sentence orders [Sch.1 para. 35(2)].

NB. An order under para.35 may repeal or amend any provision of this Part of this Act, or Chapter 1 of Part 12 Criminal Justice Act 2003 (general provisions about sentencing)[Sch.1 para. 35(3)]

Order Made by Crown Court: Direction in Relation to Further Proceedings [Sch.1 Para.36]

■ When the Crown Court makes a YRO, it may include in the order a direction that further proceedings relating to the order, be in a youth court or other magistrates' court (subject to para.7 of Schedule 2 describing the power of magistrates' courts to refer an offender to the Crown Court) [Sch.1 para. 36(1)].

NB. 'Further proceedings' referred to above, mean proceedings for any failure to comply with the order within the meaning given by para. 1(2)(b) of Schedule 2, or on any application for amendment or revocation of the order under Part 3 or 4 of that Schedule [Sch.1 para. 36(2)].

YRO: Conditions [s.1(4) & Sch.1 Para.3]

YRO with Intensive Supervision & Surveillance

■ When the conditions of s.1(4) are satisfied (see page 11), a court making a YRO which imposes an activity requirement, may specify in relation to that requirement a number of days which is more than 90 but not more than 180 [Sch.1 para.3(1)(2)].

■ Such an activity requirement is referred to in this Part of this Act as 'an extended activity requirement' [Sch.1 para.3(3)] and a YRO which imposes an extended activity requirement must also impose:

• A supervision requirement, and
• A curfew requirement (and, accordingly, if so required by para.2, an electronic monitoring requirement) [Sch.1 para.3(4)]

■ A YRO imposing an extended activity requirement (and other requirements in accordance with sub-para. (4)) is referred to in this Part of the Act as 'a YRO with intensive supervision and surveillance" (whether or not it also imposes any other requirement mentioned in s.1(1)) [Sch.1 para.3(5)].

YRO with Fostering

■ When the conditions of s.1(4) are satisfied (see page 11), a court may make a YRO in accordance with s.1

imposing a fostering requirement if it is satisfied that the:

- Behaviour which constituted the offence was due to a significant extent to the circumstances in which the offender was living, and
- Imposition of a fostering requirement (see para.18) would assist in the offender's rehabilitation [Sch.1 para.4(1);(2)]

■ But a court may not impose a fostering requirement unless it has consulted the:

- Offender's parents or guardians (unless it is impracticable to do so), and
- Local authority which is to place the offender with a local authority foster parent [Sch.1 para.4(3)]

■ A YRO which imposes a fostering requirement must also impose a supervision requirement [Sch.1 para.4(4)].

NB. Para.4 has effect subject to paras.18(7) and 19 (pre-conditions to imposing fostering requirement) [Sch.1 para.4(5)].

■ A YRO which imposes a fostering requirement is referred to in this Part of this Act as 'a YRO with fostering' (whatever other requirements mentioned in s.1(1) or (2) it imposes) [Sch.1 para.4(6)].

Intensive Supervision & Surveillance & Fostering: Further Provisions

- A YRO with intensive supervision and surveillance may not impose a fostering requirement [Sch.1 para.5(1)].

- Nothing in s.1(4)(b), or s.148(1) or (2)(b) Criminal Justice Act 2003 (restrictions on imposing community sentences), prevents a court from making a YRO with intensive supervision and surveillance in respect of an offender if the offender fails to comply with an order under s.161(2) of the Criminal Justice Act 2003 (pre-sentence drug testing) [Sch.1 para.5(2)]

NB. There is existing provision in s.152(3)(b) CJA 2003 that provides that an offender who fails to comply with a pre-sentence drug testing order under s.161(2) of that Act may be given a custodial sentence.

Schedule 2
Breach, Revocation or Amendment of YROs

Part 1: Preliminary

Interpretation [Sch.2 Paras.1–28]

- In Sch. 2, 'the offender', in relation to a YRO means the person in respect of whom the order is made [Sch.2 para. 1(1)].

- Any reference (however expressed) to an offender's compliance with a YRO is a reference to the offender's compliance with the requirement/s imposed by the order, and if the order imposes an attendance centre requirement, rules made under s.222(1)(d) or (e) Criminal Justice Act 2003 ('attendance centre rules'). Any reference (however expressed) to the offender's failure to comply with the order is a reference to any failure of the offender to comply with a requirement imposed by the order, or if the order imposes an attendance centre requirement, with attendance centre rules [Sch.2 para.1(2)].

  NB. Thus, a breach of attendance centre rules counts as a breach of the YRO which imposed the attendance centre requirement.

- For the purposes of Sch.2, a requirement falling within any paragraph of Part 2 of Sch.1 is of the same kind as any other requirement falling within that paragraph, and an electronic monitoring requirement is a requirement of the same kind as any requirement falling within Part 2 of Schedule 1 to which it relates [Sch.2 para. 1(3)].

Orders Made on Appeal [Sch.2 Para.2]

■ If a YRO has been made on appeal, for the purposes of Sch.2 it is to be treated:

- If it was made on an appeal from a magistrates' court, as having been made by a magistrates' court
- If it was made on an appeal brought from the Crown Court or from the criminal division of the Court of Appeal, as having been made by the Crown Court [Sch.2 para. 2]

Part 2: Breach of Requirement of Order

Duty to Give Warning [Sch.2 Para.3]

■ If the responsible officer is of the opinion that the offender has failed without reasonable excuse to comply with a YRO, s/he must give the offender a warning under para.3 unless, under para. 4(1) or (3) the responsible officer causes an information to be laid before a JP in respect of the failure [Sch.2 para. 3(1)].

■ A warning under para.3 must describe the circumstances of the failure, state that the failure is unacceptable, and state that the offender will be liable to be brought before a court:

• In a case where the warning is given during the warned period relating to a previous warning under this paragraph, if during that period the offender again fails to comply with the order, or

• In any other case, if during the warned period relating to the warning, the offender fails on more than 1 occasion to comply with the order [Sch.2 para. 3(2)].

■ The responsible officer must, as soon as practicable after the warning has been given, record that fact [Sch.2 para 3.(3)].

NB. In para. 3 'warned period' means the period of 12 months beginning with the date on which the warning was given[Sch.2 para. 4)].

Breach of Order [Sch.2 Para.4]

■ If the responsible officer has given a warning ('the first warning') under para. 3 to the offender in respect of a YRO, during the 'warned period' relating to the first warning, has given another warning under that paragraph to the offender in respect of a failure to comply with the order, and is of the opinion that, during the warned period relating to the first warning, the offender has again failed without reasonable excuse to comply with the order:

  • The responsible officer must cause an information to be laid before a JP in respect of the final failure mentioned above [Sch.2 para.4(1)]

■ Para. 4(1) does not apply if the responsible officer is of the opinion that there are exceptional circumstances which justify not causing an information to be so laid [Sch. 2 para.4(2)].

■ If the responsible officer is of the opinion the offender has failed without reasonable excuse to comply with a YRO and para. 4(1) (exceptional circumstances to justify not causing the information to be laid) does not apply, then s/he may cause the information to be laid before a JP in respect of that failure [Sch.2 para.4 3].

NB. Thus, a responsible officer may start court enforcement proceedings without having previously issued warnings if the breach is particularly serious.

■ 'Warned period' has the same meaning as in para. 3 [Sch.2 para.4(4))].

Issue of Summons or Warrant by JP [Sch.2 Para.5]

- If at any time while a YRO is in force it appears on information to a JP that an offender has failed to comply with it, the JP may:

  - Issue a summons requiring the offender to appear at the place and time specified in it, or
  - If the information is in writing and on oath, issue a warrant for the offender's arrest [Sch.2 para.5(1)]

- Any summons or warrant issued under para.5 must direct the offender to appear or be brought:

  - If the YRO was made by the Crown Court and does not include a direction under para.36 of Schedule 1, before the Crown Court, and
  - In any other case, before the appropriate court [Sch.2 para. 5(2)]

- 'Appropriate court' here means if the offender is aged under 18, a youth court acting in the relevant local justice area, and s/he is 18 or over, a magistrates' court (other than a youth court) acting in that local justice area [Sch.2 para.5(3)]. 'Relevant local justice area" here means the local justice area in which the offender resides, or if it is not known where s/he resides, the local justice area specified in the YRO [Sch.2 para.5(4)].

- If an offender does not appear in answer to a summons issued under para. 5, then:

  - If the summons required the offender to appear before the Crown Court, the Crown Court may, unless the summons was issued under para.5(6) issue a further summons requiring the offender to appear at the place and time specified in it, or
  - In any case, issue a warrant for the arrest of the offender [Sch.2 para.5(5)-(7)]

- If the summons required the offender to appear before a magistrates' court, the magistrates' court may issue a warrant for the arrest of the offender [Sch.2 para. 5(7)].

Power of Magistrates' Court [Sch.2 Para.6]

- Para.6 applies when:

  - An offender appears or is brought before a youth court or other magistrates' court under para.5, and
  - It is proved to the satisfaction of the court that the offender has failed without reasonable excuse to comply with the YRO [Sch.2 para.6(1)]

- The court may deal with the offender in respect of that failure in any one of the following ways:

  - By ordering the offender to pay a fine of an amount not exceeding £250 if the offender is aged under 14, or £1,000, in any other case
  - By amending the terms of the YRO so as to impose any requirement which could have been included in the order when it was made, in addition to, or in substitution for, any requirement or requirements already imposed by the order
  - By dealing with the offender, for the offence in respect of which the order was made, in any way in which the court could have dealt with the offender for that offence (had the offender been before that court to be dealt with for it) [Sch.2 para.6 (2)]

NB. If the court deals with the offender under the latter of the above provisions, it must revoke the YRO if it is still in force [Sch.2 para.6(11)].

■ Amending the terms of the YRO by addition or substitution is subject to para. 6(6) to (9) described below [Sch.2 para.6(3)].

■ In dealing with the offender under para.6(2), the court must take into account the extent to which the offender has complied with the YRO [Sch.2 para.6(4)].

■ A fine imposed under para.6(2) is to be treated, for the purposes of any enactment, as being a sum adjudged to be paid by a conviction [Sch.2 para.6(5)] and any requirement imposed under para 6(2) must be capable of being complied with before the date specified under paragraph 32(1) of Sch.1 i.e. up to 3 years after the YRO takes effect [Sch.2 para.6(6)].

■ If the court is dealing with the offender under para.6(2) and adding or substituting requirements, then Sch.1 para.10(2) applies though with the minimum number of hours reduced from 40 to 20 [Sch.2 para.6(7)].

■ The court may not under para.6(2) impose an extended activity or a fostering requirement, if the order does not already impose such a requirement [Sch.2 para.6(8)].

■ If the order imposes a fostering requirement (the 'original requirement'), and under para. (2) the court proposes to substitute a new fostering requirement (the 'substitute requirement'), para. 18(2) of Sch.1 applies in relation to the substitute requirement as if the reference to the period of 12 months beginning with the date on which the original requirement first had effect were a reference to the period of 18 months beginning with that date [Sch.2 para.6(9)].

■ If the court deals with the offender under para.6(2) and it would not otherwise have the power to amend the YRO, under para. 13 (amendment by reason of change of residence), that paragraph has effect as if references in it to the appropriate court were references to the court which is dealing with the offender [Sch.2 para.6(10)].

■ Paras. (13)–(15) apply when:

  • The court is dealing with the offender under paragraph 6(2)(c),and
  • The offender has wilfully and persistently failed to comply with a YRO [Sch.2 para.6(12)]

■ The court may impose a YRO with intensive supervision and surveillance notwithstanding anything in s.1(4)(a) or (b) [Sch.2 para.6(13)].

■ The court may impose a custodial sentence notwithstanding anything in s.152(2) Criminal Justice Act 2003 (general restrictions on imposing discretionary custodial sentences) if:

  • The order is a YRO with intensive supervision and surveillance, and

- The original offence mentioned was punishable with imprisonment [Sch.2 para.6(14)]

■ If the order is a YRO with intensive supervision and surveillance which was imposed by virtue of para.6(13) or para.8(12), and the original offence was not punishable with imprisonment, then for the purposes of dealing with the offender the court is to be taken to have had power to deal with the offender for that offence by making a detention and training order (DTO) for a term not exceeding 4 months [Sch.2 para.6(15)].

■ An offender may appeal to the Crown Court against a sentence imposed under the provisions of para.6(2) that permit the court to deal with her/him for the offence, in any way the court could have done if s/he were before it for that offence [Sch.2 para.6(16)].

Power of Magistrates' Court to Refer Offender to Crown Court [Sch.2 Para.7]

■ Para.7(2) applies if:

- The YRO was made by the Crown Court and contains a direction under para.36 of Sch.1, and
- A youth court or other magistrates' court would (apart from that subparagraph) be required, or has the power, to deal with the offender in one of the ways mentioned in para.6(2) [Sch.2 para.7(1)]

■ The court may instead commit the offender in custody, or release the offender on bail, until the offender can be brought or appear before the Crown Court [Sch.2 para.7(2)].

■ When a court deals with the offender's case under para.7(2) it must send to the Crown Court a certificate signed by a JP certifying that the offender has failed to comply with the YRO in the respect specified in the certificate, and such other particulars of the case as may be desirable, and a certificate purporting to be so signed is admissible as evidence of the failure before the Crown Court [Sch.2 para.7(3)].

Power of Crown Court [Sch.2 Para.8]

■ Para.8 applies when:

- An offender appears or is brought before the Crown Court under para. 5 or by virtue of para. 7(2), and
- It is proved to the satisfaction of that court that the offender has failed without reasonable excuse to comply with the YRO [Sch.2 para.8(1)]

■ The Crown Court may deal with the offender in respect of that failure in any one of the following ways:

- By ordering the offender to pay a fine of an amount not exceeding £250, if the offender is aged under 14, or £1,000, in any other case
- By amending the terms of the YRO so as to impose any requirement which could have been included in the order when it was made in addition to, or in substitution for, any requirement or requirements already imposed by the order
- By dealing with the offender, for the offence in respect of which the order was made, in any way in which the Crown Court could have dealt with the offender for that offence [Sch.2 para.8(2)]

■ The power to amend the terms as per the second bullet above is subject to paras.8(6) to (9) [Sch.2 para.8(3)].

- In dealing with the offender under para.8(2), the Crown Court must take into account the extent to which the offender has complied with the YRO [Sch.2 para.8(4)].

- A fine imposed under para. 8(2) is to be treated, for the purposes of any enactment, as being a sum adjudged to be paid by a conviction [Sch.2 para.8(5)].

- Any requirement imposed under para.8 (2) must be capable of being complied with before the date specified under para.32(1) of Schedule 1 i.e. 3 years from when the order takes effect [Sch.2 para.8(6)].

- When the court is dealing with the offender under para.8(2), and the YRO does not contain an unpaid work requirement, para.10(2) of Schedule 1 applies in relation to the inclusion of such a requirement as if for '40' there were substituted '20' [Sch.2 para.8(7)].

- The court may not under para.8(2) impose an extended activity requirement, or a fostering requirement, if the YRO does not already impose such a requirement [Sch.2 para.8(8)].

- If the order imposes a fostering requirement (the 'original requirement'), and under para.8 (2) the court proposes to substitute a new fostering requirement (the substitute requirement) para.18(2) of Schedule 1 applies in relation to the substitute requirement as if the reference to the period of 12 months beginning with the date on which the original requirement first had effect were a reference to the period of 18 months beginning with that date [Sch.2 para.8(9)].

■ If the Crown Court deals with an offender under the powers in para.8 (2) to deal with an offender in any way in which the Crown court could have dealt with her/him for that offence, it must revoke the YRO if it is still in force [Sch.2 para.8(10)].

■ Sch 2. para.8(12) to (14) apply when:

  • An offender has wilfully and persistently failed to comply with a YRO and
  • The Crown Court is dealing with the offender under para.8(2)(c) [Sch.2 para.8(11)]

■ The court may impose a YRO with intensive supervision and surveillance notwithstanding the first 2 criteria in s.1(4) [Sch.2 para.8(12)].

■ The court may impose a custodial sentence notwithstanding anything in s.152(2) Criminal Justice Act 2003 (general restrictions on imposing discretionary custodial sentences) if:

  • The order is a YRO with intensive supervision and surveillance, and
  • The offence mentioned in the final sub-para. of para.8(2) was punishable with imprisonment [Sch.2 para.8(13)]

■ For the purposes of dealing with the offender for the original offence, the Crown Court is to be taken to have had power to deal with the offender for that offence by making a DTO for a term not exceeding 4 months if:

- The order is a YRO with intensive supervision
- and surveillance which was imposed by virtue of para.6(13) or para.8(12) above, and
- The offence was not punishable with imprisonment [Sch.2 para.8(14)]

■ In proceedings before the Crown Court under para.8 any question whether the offender has failed to comply with the YRO is to be determined by the court and not by the verdict of a jury [Sch.2 para.8(15)].

Restriction of Powers in Paras. 6 & 8 Where Treatment Required [Sch.2 Para.9]

■ Para.9(2) applies where a YRO imposes any of the following requirements in respect of an offender:

- A mental health treatment requirement
- A drug treatment requirement
- An intoxicating substance treatment requirement [Sch.2 para.9(1)]

■ The offender is not to be treated for the purposes of paras.6 or 8 as having failed to comply with the order on the ground only that the offender had refused to undergo any surgical, electrical or other treatment required by that requirement if, in the opinion of the court, the refusal was reasonable having regard to all the circumstances [Sch.2 para.9(2)].

Power to Amend Amounts of Fines in [Sch.2 Para.10]

- The Secretary of State may by order amend any sum for the time being specified in para. 6(2) or 8(2) [Sch.2 para. 10(1)].

- The power conferred by para.10(1) may be exercised only if it appears to the Secretary of State that there has been a change in the value of money since the relevant date which justifies the change [Sch.2 para.10(2)].

  NB. The 'relevant date' here means the date on which the sum was last so substituted, or if it has not been substituted, then the date on which this Act was passed [Sch.2 para.10(3)].

- An order under para.10(1) (a 'Fine Amendment Order') must not have effect in relation to any YRO made in respect of an offence committed before the fine amendment order comes into force [Sch.2 para.10(4)].

Part 3: Revocation of Order

Revocation of Order with or without Re-sentencing: Powers of Appropriate Court [Sch.2 Para.11]

- Para. 11 applies when:

  - A YRO is in force in respect of any offender
  - The order was made by a youth court or other magistrates' court, or was made by the Crown Court and contains a direction under para.36 of Sch.1, and
  - The offender or the responsible officer makes an application to the appropriate court under this para. [Sch.2 para.11(1)]

- If it appears to the appropriate court to be in the interests of justice to do so, having regard to circumstances which have arisen since the order was made, the appropriate court may:

  - Revoke the order, or
  - Both revoke the order, and deal with the offender, for the offence in respect of which the order was made, in any way in which the appropriate court could have dealt with the offender for that offence (had the offender been before that court to be dealt with for it) [Sch.2 para.11(2)]

- The circumstances in which a YRO may be revoked under para.11(2) include the offender's making good progress or responding satisfactorily to supervision or treatment (as the case requires) [Sch.2 para.11(3)].

■ In dealing with an offender under the latter provisions of para. 11(2), the appropriate court must take into account the extent to which the offender has complied with the requirements of the YRO [Sch.2 para.11(4)].

■ A person sentenced under para.11(2) for an offence may appeal to the Crown Court against it [Sch.2 para.11(5)].

■ No application may be made by the offender under para.11(1) while an appeal against the YRO is pending [Sch.2 para.11(6)].

■ If an application under para.11 (1) relating to a YRO is dismissed, then during the period of 3 months beginning with the date on which it was dismissed no further such application may be made in relation to the order by any person except with the consent of the appropriate court [Sch.2 para.11(7)].

■ The 'appropriate court' here means if the offender is aged under 18 when the application under para.11(1) was made, a youth court acting in the local justice area specified in the YRO, and if the offender is aged 18 or over at that time, a magistrates' court (other than a youth court) acting in that local justice area [Sch.2 para.11(8)]

Revocation of Order with or without Re-sentencing: Powers of Crown Court [Sch.2 Para.12]

- Para.12 applies when:

  - A YRO is in force in respect of an offender,
  - The order was made by the Crown Court, and does not contain a direction under para. 36 of Schedule 1 that further proceedings be in a youth or magistrates' court, and
  - The offender or the responsible officer makes an application to the Crown Court under this para. [Sch.2 para.12(1)]

- If it appears to the Crown Court to be in the interests of justice to do so, having regard to circumstances which have arisen since the YRO was made, the Crown Court may:

  - Revoke the order, or
  - Both revoke the order, and deal with the offender, for the offence in respect of which the order was made, in any way in which the Crown Court could have dealt with the offender for that offence [Sch.2 para.12(2)]

- The circumstances in which a YRO may be revoked under para.12(2) include the offender's making good progress or responding satisfactorily to supervision or treatment (as the case requires) [Sch.2 para.12(3)].

■ In dealing with an offender under the latter provisions of para.12(2), the Crown Court must take into account the extent to which the offender has complied with the YRO [Sch.2 para.12(4)].

■ No application may be made by the offender under para.12(1) while an appeal against the YRO is pending [Sch.2 para.(5)].

■ If an application under para.12(1) relating to a YRO is dismissed, then during the period of 3 months beginning with the date on which it was dismissed no further such application may be made in relation to the order by any person except with the consent of the Crown Court [Sch.2 para.12(6)].

Part 4: Amendment of Order

Amendment by Appropriate Court [Sch.2 Para.13]

- Para.13 applies when:

  - A YRO is in force in respect of an offender
  - The order was made by a youth court or other magistrates' court, or was made by the Crown Court and contains a direction under para.36 of Sch.1, and
  - An application for the amendment of the order is made to the appropriate court by the offender or the responsible officer [Sch.2 para.13(1)]

- If the appropriate court is satisfied that the offender proposes to reside, or is residing, in a local justice area ('the new local justice area') other than the local justice area for the time being specified in the order, the court must, if the application under para.13(1) was made by the responsible officer, or may, in any other case, amend the YRO by substituting the new local justice area for the area specified in the order [Sch.2 para.13(2)].

  NB. Para.13(2) is subject to para.15 summarised on page 83 [Sch.2 para.13(3)].

- The appropriate court may by order amend the YRO by:

  - Cancelling any of the requirements of the order, or

- Replacing any of those requirements with a requirement of the same kind which could have been included in the order when it was made [Sch.2 para.13(4)]

NB. Para.13(4) is subject to para.16 summarised on page 85 [Sch.2 para.13(5)].

- In para.13, 'appropriate court' means:

  - If the offender is aged under 18 when the application under para.13(1) was made, a youth court acting in the local justice area specified in the YRO and
  - If the offender is aged 18 or over at that time, a magistrates' court (other than a youth court) acting in that local justice area [Sch.2 para.13(6)]

Amendment by Crown Court [Sch.2 Para.14]

- Para.14 applies when:

  - A YRO is in force in respect of an offender
  - The order was made by the Crown Court, and does not contain a direction under para.36 of Schedule 1 that further proceedings be in a youth or magistrates' court, and
  - An application for the amendment of the order is made to the Crown Court by the offender or the responsible officer [Sch.2 para.14(1)]

- If the Crown Court is satisfied the offender proposes to reside, or is residing, in a local justice area ('the new local justice area') other than the local justice area for the time being specified in the order, the court must, if the application under para.14(1) was made by the responsible officer, or may, in any other case, amend the YRO by substituting the new local justice area for the area specified in the order [Sch.2 para.14(2)].

  NB. Para,14(2) is subject to para.15 [Sch.2 para.14(3)].

- The Crown Court may by order amend the YRO by:

  - Cancelling any of the requirements of the order, or
  - Replacing any of those requirements with a requirement of the same kind which could have

been included in the order when it was made
[Sch.2 para.14(4)]

NB. Para. 14(4) is subject to Para. 16 [Sch.2 para.14(5)].

Exercise of Powers under Para.13(2) or 14(2): Further Provisions [Sch.2 Para.15]

■ In paras.15(2) and (3) below, 'specific area requirement', in relation to a YRO, means a requirement contained in the order which, in the opinion of the court, cannot be complied with unless the offender continues to reside in the local justice area specified in the order [Sch. 2 para.15(1)].

■ A court may not under para.13(2) or 14(2) amend a YRO which contains specific area requirements unless, in accordance with para.13(4) or 14(4), it either:

• Cancels those requirements, or
• Substitutes for those requirements other requirements which can be complied with if the offender resides in the new local justice area mentioned in para.13(2) or 14(2) [Sch.2 para.15(2)]

■ If an application under para.13(1) (appropriate court) or para. 14(1) Crown Court) for an amendment of the order was made by the responsible officer and the YRO contains specific requirements, the court:

• Must, unless it considers it inappropriate to do so, or is prevented from so doing by the 'area requirements' provisions of para.15(2), exercise its

powers under para.13 (4) (appropriate court) or
para.14(4) (Crown Court) [Sch.2 para.15(3)]

- The court may not under para.13(2) or 14(2) amend a
  YRO order imposing a programme requirement unless
  the court is satisfied that a programme which
  corresponds as nearly as practicable to the
  programme specified in the order for the purposes of
  that requirement, and is suitable for the offender, is
  available in the new local justice area [Sch.2
  para.15(4)].

Exercise of Powers under Para.13(4) or Para.14(4): Further Provisions [Sch.2 Para.16]

■ Any replacement of requirements imposed under para. 13(4)or 14(4) must be capable of being complied with before the date specified under para.32(1) of Sch.1 [Sch.2 para.16(1)].

■ Para.18(2) of Schedule 1 applies in relation to the substitute requirement as if the reference to the period of 12 months beginning with the date on which the original requirement first had effect were a reference to the period of 18 months beginning with that date, if:

• A YRO imposes a fostering requirement (the 'original requirement'), and
• Under para.13(4) or 14(4) a court proposes to substitute a new fostering requirement ('the substitute requirement') for the original requirement [Sch.2 para.16(2)]

■ Unless the offender has expressed willingness to comply with the requirement, the court may not under para.13(4) or 14(4) impose a:

• Mental health treatment requirement,
• Drug treatment requirement, or
• Drug testing requirement [Sch.2 para.16(3)]

■ If an offender fails to express willingness to comply with a mental health treatment requirement, a drug treatment requirement or a drug testing requirement which the court proposes to impose under para.13(4) or 14(4), the court may:

- Revoke the YRO and
- Deal with the offender, for the offence in respect of which the order was made, in any way in which that court could have dealt with the offender for that offence (had the offender been before that court to be dealt with for it) [Sch.2 para.16(4)]

NB. In dealing with the offender as above, the court must take into account the extent to which the offender has complied with the order [Sch.2 para.16(5)].

Extension of Unpaid Work Requirement [Sch.2 Para. 17]

- The court may, in relation to the order, extend the period of 12 months specified in para.10(6) of Schedule 1 if:

  - A YRO imposing an unpaid work requirement is in force in respect of an offender, and
  - On the application of the offender or the responsible officer, it appears to the appropriate court that it would be in the interests of justice to do so having regard to circumstances which have arisen since the order was made [Sch.2 para.17(1)]

Powers of Court in Relation to Order Following Subsequent Conviction

Powers of Magistrates' Court Following Subsequent Conviction [Sch.2 Para.18]

■ Para. 18 applies when:

- A YRO is in force in respect of an offender, and
- The offender is convicted of an offence (the 'further offence') by a youth court or other magistrates' court ('the convicting court') [Sch.2 para.18(1)]

■ Para.18(3) and 18(4) apply when:

- The YRO was made by a youth court or other magistrates' court, or by the Crown Court and contains a direction under para.36 of Sch.1 that further proceedings be in a youth or magistrates' court, and
- The convicting court is dealing with the offender for the further offence [Sch.2 para.18(2)]

■ The convicting court may revoke the order [Sch.2 para.18(3)].

■ When the convicting court revokes the order under para.18(3) it may deal with the offender, for the offence in respect of which the order was made, in any way in which it could have dealt with the offender for that offence (had the offender been before that court to be dealt with for the offence) [Sch.2 para.18(4)].

- The convicting court may not exercise its powers under para.18(3) or 18(4) unless it considers that it would be in the interests of justice to do so, having regard to circumstances which have arisen since the YRO was made [Sch.2 para.18(5)].

- In dealing with an offender under para.18(4), the sentencing court must take into account the extent to which the offender has complied with the order [Sch.2 para.18(6)].

- A person sentenced under para.18(4) for an offence may appeal to the Crown Court against the sentence [Sch.2 para.18(7)].

- Para.18(9) below applies when:

  - The YRO was made by the Crown Court and contains a direction under para.36 of Sch.1, and
  - The convicting court would, but for para.18(9) deal with the offender for the further offence [Sch.2 para.18(8)]

- The convicting court may, instead of proceeding under para.18(3), and until the offender can be brought before the Crown Court,:

  - Commit the offender in custody, or
  - Release the offender on bail [Sch.2 para.18(9)]

- Para.18(11) applies if the YRO was made by the Crown Court and does not contain a direction under para.36 of Sch.1 [Sch.2 para.18(10)].

■ The convicting court may, until the offender can be brought or appear before the Crown Court:

- Commit the offender in custody, or
- Release the offender on bail [Sch.2 para.18(11)]

■ When the convicting court deals with an offender's case under para.18(9) or (11), it must send to the Crown Court such particulars of the case as may be desirable [Sch.2 para.18(12)].

Powers of Crown Court Following Subsequent Conviction [Sch.2 Para.19]

- Para.19 applies when:

  - A YRO is in force in respect of an offender, and
  - The offender is convicted by the Crown Court of an offence, or is brought or appears before the Crown Court by virtue of para.18(9) or (11) or having been committed by the magistrates' court to the Crown Court for sentence [Sch.2 para.19(1)]

- The Crown Court may revoke the order [Sch.2 para.19(2)].

- If the Crown Court revokes the order under para.19 (2), it may deal with the offender, for the offence in respect of which the order was made, in any way in which the court which made the order could have dealt with the offender for that offence [Sch.2 para.19(3)].

- The Crown Court must not exercise its powers under para.19(2) or (3) unless it considers that it would be in the interests of justice to do so, having regard to circumstances which have arisen since the YRO was made [Sch.2 para.19(4)].

- In dealing with an offender under para.19(3), the Crown Court must take into account the extent to

which the offender has complied with the order
[Sch.2 para.19(5)].

- If the offender is brought or appears before the
Crown Court by virtue of para.18(9) or (11), the
Crown Court may deal with the offender for the
further offence in any way which the convicting court
could have dealt with the offender for that offence
[Sch.2 para.19(6)].

*NB. In para.19(6), 'further offence' and 'the
convicting court' have the same meanings as in
para.18 [Sch.2 para.19(7)].*

Supplementary

Appearance of Offender Before Court [Sch.2 Para.20]

■ Subject to para.20(2) below, when otherwise than on the application of the offender, a court proposes to exercise its powers under Part 3 (revocation), 4 (amendment of order) or 5 (powers of court in relation to order following subsequent conviction) of Sch.2, the court:

- Must summon the offender to appear before it and
- If the offender does not appear in answer to the summons, may issue a warrant for her/his arrest [Sch.2 para.20(1)]

■ Para.20(1) does not apply where a court proposes to make an order:

- Revoking a YRO
- Cancelling, or reducing the duration of, a requirement of a YRO or
- Substituting a new local justice area or place for one specified in a YRO [Sch.2 para.20(2)]

Warrants [Sch.2 Para.21]

■ Para.21(2) applies when an offender is arrested in pursuance of a warrant issued by virtue of Sch.2 and cannot be brought immediately before the court before which the warrant directs the offender to be brought ('the relevant court') [Sch.2 para.21(1)].

■ The person in whose custody the offender is:

  • May make arrangements for the offender's detention in a place of safety for a period of no more than 72 hours from time of the arrest, and
  • Must, within that period bring the offender before a magistrates' court [Sch.2 para.21(2)]

■ In the case of a warrant issued by the Crown Court, s.81(5) Supreme Court Act 1981(duty to bring person before magistrates' court) does not apply [Sch.2 para.21(3)].

■ A person detained under arrangements made under para.21(2) is deemed to be in legal custody [Sch.2 para.21(4)].

■ In para.21(2), a 'place of safety' has the same meaning as in the Children and Young Persons Act 1933 [Sch.2 para.21(5)].

■ Para.21(7) to (10) apply when, under para.21(2), the offender is brought before an 'alternative court' which is not the relevant court [Sch.2 para.21(6)].

■ If the relevant court is a magistrates' court:

- The alternative court may direct that the offender be released forthwith, or remand her/him, and
- For the purposes of para. (a), s.128 Magistrates' Courts Act 1980 (remand in custody or on bail) has effect as if the court referred to in subsections (1)(a), (3), (4)(a) and (5) were the relevant court [Sch.2 para.21(7)]

■ If the relevant court is the Crown Court, s.43A of that Act (functions of magistrates' court where a person in custody is brought before it with a view to appearance before the Crown Court) applies as if, in s.43A(1) the words 'issued by the Crown Court' were omitted, and the reference to s.81(5) Supreme Court Act 1981 were a reference to s.43A(2)(b) [Sch.2 para.21(8)].

■ Any power to remand the offender in custody which is conferred by s.43A or s.128 Magistrates' Courts Act 1980 is to be taken to be a power:

- If the offender is aged under 18, to remand the offender to accommodation provided by or on behalf of a local authority, and
- In any other case, to remand the offender to a prison [Sch.2 para.21(9)]

■ If the court remands the offender to accommodation provided by or on behalf of a local authority, the court must designate, as the authority which is to receive the offender, the local authority for the area in which it appears to the court that the offender resides [Sch.2 para.21(10)].

Adjournment of Proceedings [Sch.2 Para.22]

- Para.22 applies to any hearing relating to an offender held by a youth court or other magistrates' court in any proceedings under Sch.2 [Sch.2 para.22(1)].

- The court may adjourn the hearing, and, if it does so, may:
  - Direct that the offender be released forthwith, or
  - Remand the offender [Sch.2 para.22(2)]

- If the court remands the offender under para.22(2):
  - It must fix the time and place at which the hearing is to be resumed, and
  - That time and place must be the time and place at which the offender is required to appear or be brought before the court by virtue of the remand [Sch.2 para.22(3)]

- If the court adjourns the hearing under para.22(2) but does not remand the offender:
  - It may fix the time and place at which the hearing is to be resumed, but
  - If it does not do so, must not resume the hearing unless it is satisfied that the offender, the responsible officer and (if the offender is aged under 14), a parent/guardian of the offender

have had adequate notice of the time and place of the resumed hearing [Sch.2 para.22(4)]

■ The powers of a magistrates' court under para. 22 may be exercised by a single justice of the peace, notwithstanding anything in the Magistrates' Courts Act 1980 [Sch.2 para.22(5)].

■ Para. 6 applies to any hearing in any proceedings under Sch.2 in place of s.10 of Magistrates' Courts Act 1980 (adjournment of trial) where that section would otherwise apply, but is not to be taken to affect the application of that section to hearings of any other description [Sch.2 para.22(6)].

Restrictions on Imposition of Intensive Supervision & Surveillance or Fostering of Proceedings [Sch.2 Para.23]

- ■ S.1(4), and the provisions mentioned in s.1(6), apply in relation to a power conferred by para. 6(2)(b), 8(2)(b), 13(4)(b) or 14(4)(b) to impose a requirement as they apply in relation to any power conferred by s.1 or Part 1 of Schedule 1 to make a YRO which includes such a requirement [Sch.2 para.23].

Provisions of Copies of Orders etc [Sch.2 Para.24]

■ When a court makes an order under Sch.2 revoking or amending a YRO, the proper officer of the court must forthwith:

- Provide copies of the revoking or amending order to the offender and, if the offender is aged under 14, to the offender's parent or guardian
- Provide a copy of the revoking or amending order to the responsible officer
- In the case of an amending order which substitutes a new local justice area, provide copies of the amending order to the local probation board acting for that area or (as the case may be) a provider of probation services operating in that area, and the magistrates' court acting in that area
- In the case of an amending order which imposes or cancels a requirement specified in the first column of the table in para. 34(4) of Sch.1 (see page 64) provide a copy of so much of the amending order as relates to that requirement to the person specified in relation to that requirement in the second column of that table
- In the case of an order which revokes a requirement specified in the first column of that table, provide a copy of the revoking order to the person specified in relation to that requirement in the second column

- If the court is a magistrates' court acting in a local justice area other than the area specified in the YRO, provide a copy of the revoking or amending order to a magistrates' court acting in the local justice area specified in the order [Sch.2 para.24(1)]

■ If , as per the 3rd of the above roundels the proper officer of the court provides a copy of an amending order to a magistrates' court acting in a different area, s/he must also provide to that court such documents and information relating to the case as appear likely to be of assistance to a court acting in that area in the exercise of its functions in relation to the order [Sch.2 para.24(2)].

NB. In this para.24, 'proper officer' means in relation to a magistrates' court, the designated officer for the court and in relation to the Crown Court, the appropriate officer [Sch.2 para.24(3)].

Power to Amend Maximum Period of Fostering Requirement [Sch.2 Para.25]

■ The Secretary of State may by order amend para.6(9), 8(9) or 16(2) by substituting, for the period of 18 months specified in the provision, or any other period which may be so specified by virtue of a previous order under para.25 such other period as may be specified in the order [Sch.2 para.25].

Responsible Officer and Offender: Duties in Relation to the Other [s.5]

■ When a YRO has effect, it is the duty of the responsible officer to:

- Make any arrangements that are necessary in connection with the requirements imposed by the order
- Promote the offender's compliance with those requirements, and
- When appropriate, take steps to enforce those requirements [s.5(1)]

NB. In s.5(1) 'responsible officer' does not include a person falling within the first roundel of s.4(1) above [s.5(2)].

■ In giving instructions in pursuance of a YRO relating to an offender, the responsible officer must ensure, as far as practicable, that any instruction is such as to avoid any:

- Conflict with the offender's religious beliefs
- Interference with the times, if any, at which the offender normally works or attends school or any other educational establishment, and
- Conflict with the requirements of any other YRO to which the offender may be subject [s.5(3)]

■ The Secretary of State may by order provide that s.5(3) is to have effect with such additional restrictions as may be specified in the order [s.5(4)].

■ An offender in respect of whom a YRO is in force
  must:

  • Keep in touch with the responsible officer in
    accordance with such instructions as the offender
    may from time to time be given by that officer,
    and
  • Notify the responsible officer of any change of
    address [s.5(5)]

■ The obligation imposed by s.5(5) is enforceable as if
  it were a requirement imposed by the order [s.5(6)].

PART 2

SENTENCING

General Sentencing Provisions

Purposes etc of Sentencing: Offenders Under 18 [s.9]

■ S.9 inserts after s.142 Criminal Justice Act 2003 (CJA 2003) a new s.142A (purposes etc. of sentencing: offenders under 18). S.142A applies when a court is dealing with an offender aged under 18 in respect of an offence [s.142A(1) CJA 2003].

■ The court must have regard to:

  • The principal aim of the youth justice system (which is to prevent offending (or re-offending) by persons aged under 18) – see s.37(1) Crime and Disorder Act 1998
  • In accordance with s.44 Children and Young Persons Act 1933, the welfare of the offender, and
  • The purposes of sentencing mentioned in s.142A(3) below (so far as it is not required to do so by the first of the above bullet points) [s.142A(2) CJA 2003]

■ Those purposes of sentencing are the:

  • Punishment of offenders
  • Reform and rehabilitation of offenders
  • Protection of the public, and
  • Making of reparation by offenders to persons affected by their offences [s.142A(3) CJA 2003]

■ S.142A does not apply:

- To an offence the sentence for which is fixed by law
- To an offence the sentence for which falls to be imposed under s.51A(2) Firearms Act 1968 (minimum sentence for certain firearms offences), s.29(6) Violent Crime Reduction Act 2006 (minimum sentences in certain cases of using someone to mind a weapon) or s.226(2) of this Act (detention for life for certain dangerous offenders), or
- In relation to the making under Part 3 of the Mental Health Act 1983 of a hospital order (with or without a restriction order), an interim hospital order, a hospital direction or a limitation direction [s.142A(4) CJA 2003]

NB. In s.44 Children and Young Persons Act 1933 (general considerations) after s.44(1) insert a s.1A indicating that s.44(1) is to be read with paragraphs (a) and (c) of s.142A(2) Criminal Justice Act 2003 (which require a court dealing with an offender aged under 18 also to have regard to the principal aim of the youth justice system and the specified purposes of sentencing). Accordingly, in determining in the case of an offender whether it should take steps as mentioned in s.142A(1) the court shall also have regard to the matters mentioned in those paragraphs.

Pre-Sentence Reports [s.12]

- S.12 inserts after s.158 Criminal Justice Act 2003 (meaning of 'pre-sentence report'), the following:

  - Subject to any rules made under ss.158(1)(b) and to s.158(1B), the court may accept a pre-sentence report given orally in open court [s.158(1A) CJA 2003]
  - But a pre-sentence report relating to an offender aged under 18 and required to be obtained and considered before the court forms an opinion mentioned in s.156(3)(a), must be in writing [s.158(1B) CJA 2003]

Custodial Sentences

Extended Sentences for Certain Violent or Sexual Offences: Persons Under 18 [s.16]

■ S.228 Criminal Justice Act 2003 (extended sentence for certain violent or sexual offences: persons under 18) is amended to the effect that:

- Courts now have a power rather than a duty to impose an extended sentence
- This power may only be exercised when the immediate offence would attract an appropriate custodial term of a minimum of 4 years

NB. S.16(6) gives the Secretary of State a power to substitute a different period for the above 4 years minimum.

Referral Orders

Referral Conditions [s.35]

- S.35 amends s.17 Powers of Criminal Courts (Sentencing) Act 2000 which sets out the circumstances in which a magistrates' court must or may impose a Referral Order when sentencing a child/young person. If the child/young person is given such an order s/he is required to attend a youth offender panel which consists of 2 volunteers from the local community and a panel adviser from a YOT. The panel, young person, parent/carer/s and (if appropriate, the victim) agree a contract of between 3 and 12 months with the aim of preventing re-offending.

- S.35(2) amends s.17(1) Powers of Criminal Courts (Sentencing) Act 2000 so as to remove the condition that the offender must never have been bound over to keep the peace. Thus, the fact that an offender has previously been bound over to keep the peace would not be a bar on the making of a mandatory Referral Order.

- S.35(3) inserts a new s.17(2) into the Powers of Criminal Courts (Sentencing) Act 2000 the effect of which is to modify the conditions that must be met before a discretionary Referral Order can be made.

- The fact that the offender has previously been bound over to keep the peace is no longer a bar to making a discretionary Referral Order. It is now also possible to make a discretionary order when the offender had 1 previous conviction and when, in respect of that conviction, a Referral Order had not been made. A 2nd Referral Order is also possible in exceptional circumstances where this has been recommended by an appropriate officer.

NB. S.35(4) repeals s.17(5) Powers of Criminal Courts (Sentencing) Act 2000 which means that a conditional discharge is no longer treated as a conviction for the purpose of s.17 of that Act.

Power to Revoke a Referral Order [s.36]

■ Part 3 of the Powers of Criminal Courts (Sentencing) Act 2000 (mandatory and discretionary referral of young offenders) is amended by s.36 by means of the insertion of a s.27A, so that a power is provided for a youth offender panel to refer the offender back to the appropriate court if they consider it is in the interests of justice for the Referral Order to be revoked e.g. because the offender has made good progress or when there are other reasons to do so.

Extension of Period for Which Young Offender Contract Has Effect [s.37]

- Part 3 Powers of Criminal Courts (Sentencing) Act 2000 (mandatory and discretionary referral of young offenders) is amended by the insertion of a s.27B and a new Part into Sch.1 (further court proceedings).

- The net effect of the above changes is that:

  - There is now a power for the youth offender panel to refer the offender back to the appropriate court if they consider it is in the interests of justice for the period of the Referral Order to be extended
  - The court may extend the period of the order by up to 3 months subject to the overarching maximum for a Referral Order of 12 months.

Enforcement of Sentences

Imposition of Unpaid Work Requirement for Breach of Community Order [s.38]

- Paras. 9 and 10 of Schedule 8 Criminal Justice Act 2003 (breach of community order) are amended as follows.

- If the magistrates' or Crown Court deals with an offender by amending the terms of a Community Order and imposing more onerous requirements (and when the order does not already contain an unpaid work requirement), the minimum period of unpaid work is reduced from 40 to 20 hours.

  NB. If a Community Order already contains an unpaid work requirement, there is no minimum amount by which the period of unpaid work may be increased. Unchanged are the provisions for a 40 hour minimum of unpaid work that may be imposed as a requirement of a Community Order at the point of sentence, or the existing maximum of 300 hours of unpaid work, whether imposed as a sentence or for breach.

Youth Default Orders [s.39]

■ S.39(2) applies in any case when, in respect of a person aged under 18, a magistrates' court would, but for s.89 Powers of Criminal Courts (Sentencing) Act 2000 (restrictions on custodial sentences), have power to issue a warrant of commitment for default in paying a sum adjudged to be paid by a conviction e.g. a fine (other than a sum ordered to be paid under s.6 Proceeds of Crime Act 2002) [s.39(1)] e.g. enforcement proceedings against a parent/guardian under s.81 Magistrates' Courts Act 1981.

■ The magistrates' court may, instead of proceeding under s.81 Magistrates' Courts Act 1980 (enforcement of fines imposed on young offender), order the person in default to comply with:

- In the case of a person of 16 or 17, an unpaid work requirement (see para.10 of Sch.1 on page 20)
- An attendance centre requirement (see para.12 of that Schedule) or
- A curfew requirement (see para. 14 of that Schedule).

NB. In s.39 and Sch. 7, a 'Youth Default Order' means an order under s.39(2)[s.39(3)].

■ S.1(2) and para. 2 of Sch. 1 (power or requirement to impose electronic monitoring requirement) have effect in relation to a Youth Default Order as they

have effect in relation to a Youth Rehabilitation
Order [s.39(4)].

■ When a magistrates' court has power to make a
Youth Default Order, it may, if it thinks it expedient
to do so, postpone the making of the order until such
time and on such conditions (if any) as it thinks just
[s.39(5)].

■ The following provisions have effect in relation to
Youth Default Orders as they have effect in relation
to Youth Rehabilitation Orders, subject to the
modifications of in Sch.7 (not detailed in this guide).

- S.4 (meaning of responsible officer), s.5
(responsible officer and offender: duties in
relation to the other) and s.7 (Youth
Rehabilitation Orders: interpretation)
- Paras.1, 10, 12, 14, 26, 27, 29, 33 and 34 of
Sch.1 (Youth Rehabilitation Orders: further
provisions),
- Sch. 2 (breach, revocation or amendment of
Youth Rehabilitation Orders), and
- Sch.3 (transfer of youth rehabilitation orders to
Northern Ireland, not covered in this guide
[s.39(6)]

■ If a Youth Default Order has been made for default in
paying any sum:

- On payment of the whole sum to any person
authorised to receive it, the order ceases to have
effect, and

- On payment of a part of the sum to any such person, the total number of hours or days to which the order relates is to be taken to be reduced
- by a proportion corresponding to that which the part paid bears to the whole sum [s.39(7)]

NB. In calculating any reduction required by the latter of the above bullet points, any fraction of a day or hour is to be disregarded [s.39(8)].

Power to Impose Attendance Centre Requirement on Fine Defaulter [s.40]

- S.300 Criminal Justice Act 2003 (power to impose unpaid work requirement or curfew requirement on fine defaulter) is amended so that the option of an attendance centre requirement is added when the offender is aged under 25.

Disclosure of Information for Enforcing Fines [s.41]

- Schedule 5 to the Courts Act 2003 (attachment of earnings orders and applications for benefit deductions) is amended as follows by the insertion of paras. 9A, 9B and 9C [s.41(1)].

Disclosure of Information in Connection with Application for Benefit Reductions [Para.9A Courts Act 2003]

- The designated officer for a magistrates' court may make an information request to the Secretary of State for the purpose of facilitating the making of a decision by the court as to whether it is practicable or appropriate to make an application for benefit deductions in respect of P [para. 9A(1)].

- An information request is a request for the disclosure of some or all of the following information:

  - P's full name
  - P's address (or any of P's addresses)
  - P's date of birth
  - P's national insurance number
  - P's benefit status [para.9A(2)]

- On receiving an information request, the Secretary of State may disclose the information requested to:

  - The officer who made the request, or

- A justices' clerk specified in the request [para.9A(3)]

Restrictions on Disclosure [Para.9B Courts Act 2003]

- A person to whom information is disclosed under para. 9A(3), or 9B(1), may disclose the information to any person to whom its disclosure is necessary or expedient in connection with facilitating the making of a decision by the court as to whether it is practicable or appropriate to make an application for benefit deductions in respect of P [para.9B(1)].

- A person to whom such information is disclosed commits an offence if the person:

  - Discloses or uses the information, and
  - The disclosure is not authorised by para.9B(1) or (as the case may be) the use is not for the purpose of facilitating the making of such a decision as is mentioned in that subparagraph [para.9B(2)]

- But it is not an offence under para.9B(2) to disclose any information:

  - In accordance with any enactment or order of a court or for the purposes of any proceedings before a court; or
  - Which has previously been lawfully disclosed to the public [para.9B(3)]

■ It is a defence for a person charged with an offence under para.9B(2) to prove that the person reasonably believed that the disclosure or use was lawful [para.9B(3)].

■ A person guilty of an offence under para.9B(2) is liable on summary conviction to a fine not exceeding level 4 on the standard scale [para.9B(4)].

Paras.9A & 9B: Supplementary [Para.9C Courts Act 2003]

■ For the purposes of paras. 9A and 9B 'benefit status means whether or not P is in receipt of any prescribed benefit or benefits and, if so (in the case of each benefit):

- Which benefit it is
- If is already subject to deductions under any enactment, the nature of the deductions concerned, and
- The amount received by P by way of the benefit, after allowing for any such deductions

■ 'Information' means information held in any form and 'Prescribed' means prescribed by regulations made by the Lord Chancellor [para.9C(1)-(4)].

NB. Nothing in paragraph 9A or 9B authorises the making of a disclosure which contravenes the Data Protection Act 1998 [para.9C(5)].

PART 4

OTHER CRIMINAL JUSTICE PROVISIONS

Alternatives to Prosecution

Alternatives to Prosecution for Offenders under 18 [s.48]

- Sch.9 amends the Crime and Disorder Act 1998 to make:

  - Provision for the giving of 'youth conditional cautions' to children and young persons, and
  - Minor amendments relating to reprimands and warnings under s.65 of that Act [s.48(1)]

- The Secretary of State may by order amend the Crime and Disorder Act 1998 as amended by Sch.9, so as to vary the provision made by it for the giving of youth conditional cautions to children and young persons under the age of 16 (including doing so by adding or omitting any provision) [s.48(2)].

  NB. Thus, s.49 and Sch.9 extend the adult conditional caution scheme of Part 3 of the Criminal Justice Act 2003 to young offenders.

Reprimands/ Warnings

Reprimands & Warnings [s.65(1) CDA 1998 as amended by Sch.9 CJIA 2008]

■ Before a police officer can issue a reprimand or a warning, the following 5 criteria must be satisfied the:

- Police have evidence that a child/young person (the offender) has committed an offence
- Police consider there is sufficient evidence to charge the offender with the offence
- Offender admits to police s/he has committed the offence
- Offender has not previously been convicted of an offence or given a youth conditional caution in respect of an offence and
- Police do not consider that the offender should be prosecuted or given a youth conditional caution

■ When the offender has not previously been reprimanded or warned police may reprimand her/him.

■ The police may warn the offender if:

- S/he has not previously been warned or
- The offence was committed more than 2 years after the date of previous warning and they do not consider the offence serious enough to require a charge to be brought or a youth

conditional caution to be given [s.65(3) CDA 1998]

NB. No defendant may have a 2nd warning under s.65(3) (itself an exception to the general rule that nobody may be warned more than once), i.e. even if another 2 years elapsed, a 3rd warning could not be issued.

■ If the offender has not been previously reprimanded but police consider the offence serious enough, they must warn rather than reprimand her/him [s.65 (4) CDA 1998].

No previous reprimand or warning	police *may* reprimand
No previous warning or offence more than 2 years after date of previous warning	police *may* warn
No previous reprimand but police consider offence serious enough to require a warning	police *must* warn rather than reprimand

■ The police are obliged:

- If the offender is under 17, administer the reprimand or warning in the presence of an appropriate adult
- To explain to the offender (and when relevant the appropriate adult) in ordinary language the effects of reprimands and warnings respectively on any future offences within 2 years as per s.66 explained below [s.65(5) CDA 1998]

NB. For the above purposes, an appropriate adult means a parent/guardian; if in the care of a local authority or voluntary organisation a representative of that organisation; a social worker of a local authority social services department, or, if none of these is available, any responsible person aged 18 or over who is not a police officer or employed by the police [s.65(7) CDA 1998].

■ No caution, other than a youth conditional caution, can be given to a child or young person [s.65(8) as substituted by Sch.9 para.2(6)]

■ The Secretary of State is obliged to publish guidance on give reprimands or warnings e.g. seriousness of offence, rank of police officer to administer them, the form they should take etc.[s.65(6) CDA 1998]

Effects [s.66 CDA 1998]

■ When police warn an offender they must, as soon as practicable refer her/him to a YOT [s.66 (1) CDA 1998].

■ A YOT must assess any such person and unless they consider it inappropriate to do so, must arrange for her/him to participate in a rehabilitation programme [s.66 (2) CDA 1998].

NB. The Secretary of State must issue guidance about what is to be included in such rehabilitation programmes, the manner in which any failure by a person to participate in such a programme is to be recorded and the person to who any such failure is to be notified [s.66(3) CDA 1998].

- When a person who has received a warning under s.65 is convicted of an offence committed within 2 years of the warning, the court:

  - Cannot grant a conditional discharge for the offence unless it is of the opinion that there are exceptional circumstances relating to the offence/offender which justify it (and where it does so, must state in open court it is of that opinion and why) [s.66(4) CDA 1998 as amended by Sch.9 para.198 PCCSA 2000]

NB. Any reprimand, warning or failure to participate in a rehabilitation programme arrange for her/him under s.65 may be cited in criminal proceedings in the same circumstances as conviction of the person may be cited [s.66(5) CDA 1998].

Youth Conditional Cautions

Youth Conditional Cautions [s.66A CDA 1998 as inserted by Sch.9 Para.3 CJIA 2008]

■ An authorised person may give a youth conditional caution to a child/young person (the offender) if:

- The offender has not previously been convicted of an offence, and
- Each of the 5 requirements in s.66B is satisfied [s.66A(1) CDA 1998]

NB. 'Youth conditional caution' means a caution given in respect of an offence committed by the offender and which has conditions attached to it with which the offender must comply [s.66A(2) CDA 1998].

■ The conditions which may be attached to such a caution are those which have 1 or more of the following objects:

- Facilitating the rehabilitation of the offender
- Ensuring that the offender makes reparation for the offence
- Punishing the offender [s.66A(3)]

■ The conditions that may be attached to a youth conditional caution include:

- (Subject to s.66C) a condition that the offender pay a financial penalty

- A condition that the offender attend at a specified place at specified times ('specified' means specified by a relevant prosecutor) [s.66A(4)]

■ The conditions in s.66(4) may not require the offender to attend for more than 20 hours in total, not including any attendance required by conditions attached for the purpose of facilitating the offender's rehabilitation [s.66A(5)].

NB. The Secretary of State may by order amend s.66A(5) by substituting a different figure [s.66A(6)] and in s.66A, an 'authorised person' means a constable, investigating officer, or a person authorised by a relevant prosecutor for the purposes of this section [s.66A(7)].

The 5 Requirements [s.66B CDA 1998 as inserted by Sch.9 Para.3 CJIA 2008]

■ The first requirement is that the authorised person has evidence that the offender has committed an offence [s.66B(1)].

■ The second requirement is that a relevant prosecutor decides:

- There is sufficient evidence to charge the offender with the offence, and
- A youth conditional caution should be given to the offender in respect of the offence [s.66B(2)]

■ The third requirement is that the offender admits to the authorised person that s/he committed the offence [s.66B(3)].

■ The fourth requirement is that the authorised person explains the effect of the youth conditional caution to the offender and warns her/him that failure to comply with any of the conditions attached to the caution may result in her/him being prosecuted for the offence [s.66B(4)].

■ If the offender is aged 16 or under, the explanation and warning mentioned in s.66B(4) must be given in the presence of an appropriate adult.

■ The fifth requirement is that the offender signs a document which contains:

- Details of the offence
- An admission by her/him that s/he committed the offence
- Her/his consent to being given the youth conditional caution, and
- The conditions attached to the caution [s.66B(6)]

Financial Penalties [s.66C CDA 1998 as inserted by Sch.9 Para.3 CJIA 2008]

■ A condition that the offender pay a financial penalty (a 'financial penalty condition') may not be attached to a youth conditional caution given in respect of an offence unless the offence is one that is prescribed, or of a description prescribed, in an order made by the Secretary of State [s.66C(1)].

■ An order under s.66C(1) must prescribe, in respect of each offence or description of offence in the order, the maximum amount of the penalty that may be specified under s.66C(5) [s.66C(2)].

■ The amount that may be prescribed in respect of any offence must not exceed £100 [s.66C(3)].

■ The Secretary of State may by order amend s.66C(3) by substituting a different figure [s.66C(4)].

■ If a financial penalty condition is attached to a youth conditional caution, a relevant prosecutor must also specify:

• The amount of the penalty, and
• The person to whom the financial penalty is to be paid and how it may be paid [s.66C(5)]

NB. To comply with the condition, the offender must pay the penalty in accordance with the provision specified under s.66C(5)[s.66C(6)] and if a financial penalty is (in accordance with the provision specified under s.66C(5) paid to a person other than a designated officer for a local justice area, the person to whom it is paid must give the payment to such an officer [s.66C(7)]

Variation of Conditions [s.66D CDA 1998 as inserted by Sch.9 Para.3 CJIA 2008]

■ A relevant prosecutor may, with the consent of the offender, vary the conditions attached to a youth conditional caution by:

- Modifying or omitting any of the conditions
- Adding a condition [s.66D]

Failure to Comply with Conditions [s.66E CDA 1998 as inserted by Sch.9 Para.3 CJIA 2008]

■ If the offender fails, without reasonable excuse, to comply with any of the conditions attached to the youth conditional caution, criminal proceedings may be instituted against the person for the offence in question [s.66E(1)].

■ The document mentioned in s.66B(6) is to be admissible in such proceedings [s.66E(2)].

■ When such proceedings are instituted, the youth conditional caution is to cease to have effect [s.66E(3)].

■ S.24A(1) Criminal Justice Act 2003 ('the 2003 Act') applies in relation to the conditions attached to a youth conditional caution as it applies in relation to the conditions attached to a conditional caution (within the meaning of Part 3 of that Act) [s.66E(4)].

■ S.24A(2) to (9) and s.24B of the 2003 Act apply in relation to a person arrested under s.24A(1) of that Act by virtue of s.66E(4) above as they apply in relation to a person who is arrested under that section for failing to comply with any of the conditions attached to a conditional caution (within the meaning of Part 3 of that Act) [s.66E(5)].

Restrictions on Sentencing Powers Where Youth Conditional Caution Given [s.66F CDA 1998 as inserted by Sch.9 Para.3 CJIA 2008]

■ When a person who has been given a youth conditional caution is convicted of an offence committed within 2 years of the giving of the caution, the court by or before which the person is so convicted:

  • May not make an order under s.12(1)(b) Powers of Criminal Courts (Sentencing) Act 2000 (conditional discharge) in respect of the offence unless it is of the opinion that there are exceptional circumstances relating to the offence or the offender which justify its doing so; and
  • If it does make such an order, must state in open court that it is of that opinion and why it is [s.66F]

Code of Practice on Youth Conditional Cautions [s.66G CDA 1998 as inserted by Sch.9 Para.3 CJIA 2008]

■ The Secretary of State must prepare a code of practice in relation to youth conditional cautions [s.66G(1)].

■ The code may, in particular, make provision as to:

  • The circumstances in which youth conditional cautions may be given
  • The procedure to be followed in connection with the giving of such cautions

- The conditions which may be attached to such cautions and the time for which they may have effect
- The category of constable or investigating officer by whom such cautions may be given
- The persons who may be authorised by a relevant prosecutor for the purposes of s.66A
- The form which such cautions are to take and the manner in which they are to be given and recorded
- The places where such cautions may be given
- The provision which may be made by a relevant prosecutor under the second of the criteria in s.66C(5)
- The monitoring of compliance with conditions attached to such cautions
- The exercise of the power of arrest conferred by s.24A(1) Criminal Justice Act 2003 as it applies by virtue of s.66E(4)
- Who is to decide how a person should be dealt with under s.24A(2) of that Act as it applies by virtue of s.66E(5) [s.66G(2)]

■ After preparing a draft of the code the Secretary of State must publish a draft, consider any representations made to her/him about it and may amend the draft accordingly though s/he may not publish or amend the draft without the consent of the Attorney General [s.s.66G(3)].

■ After the Secretary of State has proceeded under s.66G(3) s/he must lay the code before each House of Parliament [s.66G(4)].

■ When s/he has done so s/he may bring the code into force by order [s.66G(5)].

■ The Secretary of State may from time to time revise a code of practice brought into force under s.66G [s.66G(6)].

NB. S.66G(3) to (6) apply (with appropriate modifications) to a revised code as they apply to an original code[s.66G(7)].

PART 8

ANTI-SOCIAL BEHAVIOUR

Anti-social Behaviour

NB. To render more meaningful, the new provisions about reviews of ASBOs (see below) the following material summarises the criteria and process for their making, their effect, duration, variation, breaches and appeals.

Anti-Social Behaviour Orders (ASBOs) [s.1; 1A CDA 1998 as amended by s.85 ASBA 2003]

■ An application for an order under this section may be made by a relevant authority i.e. the council for a local government area, (in England) County Council, any chief officer of police for the area, chief constable of British Transport Police Force, any person registered as a social landlord or a Housing Action Trust if it appears to them that the conditions described below are fulfilled with respect to any person aged 10 or over [s.1(1A) CDA 1998 as amended by s.61(1) PRA 2002 and s.85 ASBA 2003]

NB. The Secretary of State now has the power to enable non-Home Office Police Forces and such bodies as Transport for London and the Environment Agency to apply for Anti Social Behaviour Orders [s.1A as inserted by s.62 PRA 2002].

Conditions [s.1 (1) (a) & (b) CDA 1998 as amended by s.61 (2) PRA 2002]

■ The conditions are that:

• The person has, since the section's commencement on 01.04.99 [SI 1998/3263] acted in an anti-social manner i.e. a manner that caused or was likely to cause harassment, alarm or distress to one or more persons not of the same household as her/himself and

- Such an order is necessary to protect 'relevant' persons in the local government area in which the harassment, alarm or distress was caused or was likely to be caused; in the police area or area policed by the British Transport police, or premises provided or managed by the social landlord/Housing Action Trust from further anti-social acts by her/him.

■ Such an application must be made by complaint to the magistrates' court [s.1 (3) CDA 1998 as amended by s.61 (6) PRA 2002 and s.85(3) ASBA 2003].

■ If on application, it is proved that the conditions mentioned in s.1 (1) are fulfilled the magistrates' court may make an 'Anti Social Behaviour Order' (ASBO) under this section [s.1 (4) CDA 1998].

NB. For the purposes of determining whether the 'anti-social manner' criterion of s.1 (1) (a) is satisfied the court must disregard any act of the defendant which s/he shows was reasonable in the circumstances [s.1 (5) CDA 1998].

s.1B CDA 1998 introduced by s.63 PRA 2002 enables relevant authorities to apply to the County Court in certain circumstances for an ASBO.

Effect of Anti Social Behaviour Order [s.1 (4) & (6) as substituted by s.61 (7) PRA 2002]

- The above order prohibits the defendant from doing anything described in the order.

- Prohibitions are those necessary for the purpose of protecting from further anti-social acts by defendant, relevant persons elsewhere in England and Wales.

Consultation Requirements [s.1E CDA 1998 as inserted by s.66 PRA 2002]

- A council of a local government area must consult the chief officer of police with jurisdiction in that area before applying for an ASBO.

- Similarly, a chief officer of police must consult the council of the local government area before s/he initiates an application.

- British Transport police and registered social landlords/Housing Action Trusts must consult both the appropriate council and police.

Interim Orders [s.1D CDA 1998 as inserted by s.65 PRA 2002]

- A magistrates' court or the County Court is able to make an interim order under s.1 or new s.1B before the application process is complete, if the court considers it just to do so [s.1D(1) CDA 1998].

  NB. Interim orders are not available to criminal courts because orders under s.1C (see below) can only be made in the criminal courts once the case is complete and the offender has been convicted.

Duration of Anti-Social Behaviour Order [s.1 (7) CDA 1998]

■ The order will have effect for a period not less than 2 years which is specified in the order, or until further order is made.

Variation or Discharge of Anti-Social Behaviour (including interim) Order [s.1 (8) & (9) CDA 1998]

■ Except by the consent of both parties, no ASBO will be discharged before the end of the 2 years beginning with the date of its service [s.1 (9) CDA 1998].

NB. The consent provision does not apply to an order under s.1C in criminal proceedings (see below).

■ The applicant or the defendant may apply by complaint to the court which made an ASBO for it to be varied or discharged by a further order [s.1 (8) CDA 1998].

Breach of Anti-Social Behaviour (including interim) Order [s.1 (10) & (11) CDA 1998 as amended]

■ If, without reasonable excuse a person does anything which s/he is prohibited from doing by an ASBO, s/he is guilty of an offence and liable:

- On summary conviction, to imprisonment for up to 6 months or a fine not exceeding the statutory maximum, or both
- On conviction on indictment, to imprisonment for up to 5 years or a fine [s.1 (10)]

NB. A person convicted of such a breach cannot be given a conditional discharge under s.12 PCCSA 2000 [s.1 (11) CDA 1998].

Appeal against Anti-Social Behaviour (including interim) Order [s.4 CDA 1998]

- An appeal against an ASBO made by the magistrates' court will be heard by the Crown Court.

- On such an appeal, the Crown Court may:

  - Make such orders as may be necessary to give effect to its determination of the appeal and
  - Also make such incidental or consequential orders as appear to it to be just

  NB. Any order of the Crown Court made on an appeal under s.4 CDA 1998 (other than one directing an application be re-heard by the magistrates' court) must, for purposes of future variation or discharge applications be treated as if an order of the magistrates' court from which appeal was brought and not an order of the Crown Court.

- If an ASBO is made in respect of a person aged under 16, the court which makes the order must make a Parenting Order if it is satisfied that the relevant condition is fulfilled or if it is not so satisfied, must state in open court that it is not and why it is not [s. 9(1B) CDA 1998].

Review of Anti-social Behaviour Orders etc [s.123]

- s.123 inserts, in Part 1 of the Crime and Disorder Act 1998 (prevention of crime and disorder) and after section 1I, a new s.1J (review of orders under ss.1, 1B and 1C [s.123(1)]) and a new s.1K (responsibility for and participation in reviews under s.1J).

Review of Orders Under ss.1,1B & 1C

- S.123 applies when an ASBO, order under s.1B, or order under s.1C CDA 1998 has been made in respect of a person under the age of 17 [s.1J(1) CDA 1998 as inserted by s.123 CJIA 2008].

- If the person subject to the order will be under the age of 18 at the end of the 'review period' specified in s.1J(3) and the term of the order runs until the end of that period or beyond, then before the end of that period a review of the operation of the order shall be carried out [s.1J(2) CDA 1998 as inserted by s.123 CJIA 2008].

- The review periods are the period of 12 months beginning with the day:

  - On which the order was made, or if during that period there is one or more supplemental order, the date of the supplemental order (or the last of them)
  - After the end of the previous review period, or

- if during that period there is one or more supplemental order the date of the supplemental order (or the last of them) [s.1J(3) CDA 1998 as inserted by s.123 CJIA 2008]

■ In s.1J (3) 'supplemental order' means a further order varying the order in question or an ISO (ISO) made in relation to the order in question on an application under s.1AA(1A)[s.1J(4) CDA 1998 as inserted by s.123 CJIA 2008].

NB. S.1J (2) does not apply in relation to any review period if the order is discharged before the end of that period [s.1J(5) CDA 1998 as inserted by s.123 CJIA 2008].

■ A review under s.1J shall include consideration of:

- The extent to which the person subject to the order has complied with it
- The adequacy of any support available to the person to help her/him comply with it
- Any matters relevant to the question whether an application should be made for the order to be varied or discharged [s.1J(6) CDA 1998 as inserted by s.123 CJIA 2008]

■ Those carrying out or participating in a review under s.1J shall have regard to any guidance issued by the Secretary of State when considering:

- How the review should be carried out
- What particular matters should be dealt with by the review

- What action (if any) it would be appropriate to take in consequence of the findings of the review [s.1J(7) CDA 1998 as inserted by s.123 CJIA 2008]

Responsibility for and Participation in Reviews Under s.1J

- A review under s.1J of an ASBO or an order under s.1B shall be carried out by the relevant authority that applied for the order [s.1K(1) CDA 1998 as inserted by s.123 CJIA 2008].

- A review under s.1J of an order under s.1C shall be carried out by the appropriate chief officer of police except when a relevant authority is specified under s.1C(9ZA) when it is to be carried out by that authority [s.1K(2) CDA 1998 as inserted by s.123 CJIA 2008].

- A local authority, in carrying out a review under s.1J, shall act in co-operation with the appropriate chief officer of police; and it shall be the duty of that chief officer to co-operate in the carrying out of the review [s.1K(3) CDA 1998 as inserted by s.123 CJIA 2008].

- The chief officer of police of a police force, in carrying out a review under s.1J, shall act in co-operation with the appropriate local authority; and it shall be the duty of that local authority to co-operate in the carrying out of the review [s.1K(4) CDA 1998 as inserted by s.123 CJIA 2008].

- A relevant authority other than a local authority or chief officer of police, in carrying out a review under s.1J shall act in cooperation with the appropriate local authority and appropriate chief officer of police, and it is the duty of that local authority and chief officer to co-operate in the carrying out of the review [s.1K(5) CDA 1998 as inserted by s.123 CJIA 2008].

■ A chief officer of police or other relevant authority carrying out a review under s.1J may invite the participation in the review of a person or body not required by s.1K(3), (4) or (5) to co-operate in the carrying out of the review [s.1K(6) CDA 1998 as inserted by s.123 CJIA 2008]

■ In s.1K, the 'appropriate chief officer of police' means the chief officer of the police force maintained for the police area in which the person subject to the order resides or appears to reside, 'appropriate local authority' means the council for the local government area (as per s.1(12)) in which the person subject to the order resides or appears to reside [s.1K(7) CDA 1998 as inserted by s.123 CJIA 2008].

NB. Para.23 of Sch.27 (transitional etc provisions) sets out the timing criteria for ASBOs to be subject of the new review requirement. In addition to all the requirements above, a reviewable ASBO must be less than 9 months old when those provisions come into force or have been varied 9 months or less before the requirement comes into force.

Individual Support Orders

Individual Support Orders (ISOs) [s.1AA CDA 1998 introduced by s.322 CJA 2003 and amended by s.124 CJIA 2008]

Effect and Duration [s.1AA as amended]

■ S.1AA applies when a court makes an ASBO in respect of a defendant who is a child or young person when that order is made.

■ S.1AA also applies when:

- An ASBO has previously been made in respect of such a defendant
- An application is made complaint to the court which made that order by the relevant authority which applied for it, for an order under s.1AA and
- At the time of the hearing of the application, the defendant is still a child/young person and the ASBO is still in force [s.1AA(1);(2) CDA 1998 as substituted by s.124 CJIA 2008]

■ The court must consider whether the individual support conditions are fulfilled, and if satisfied that they are, make an ISO which:

- Requires the defendant to comply, for a period not exceeding 6 months, with such requirements as are specified in the order, and
- Requires the defendant to comply with any directions given by the responsible officer with a

view to the implementation of the above requirements [s.1AA(1B) CDA 1998 as substituted by s.124(2) CJIA 2008]

Condition for Making an ISO [s.1AA (3) CDA 1998 as amended]

- The individual support conditions are that:

  - Such an order would be desirable in the interests of preventing any repetition of the kind of behaviour which led to the ASBO or an order varying it (in a case when the variation is made as a result of further anti-social behaviour by the defendant)
  - The defendant is not already subject to an ISO, and
  - The court has been notified by the Secretary of State that arrangements for implementing ISOs are available in the area in which it appears to it that the defendant resides or will reside and the notice has not been withdrawn

- If the court is not satisfied that the individual support conditions are fulfilled, it shall state in open court that it is not so satisfied and why it is not [s.1AA(4) CDA 1998]

- The requirements that may be specified under s.1AA (2)(a) are those that the court considers desirable in the interests of preventing any repetition of the kind of behaviour which led to the making of the ASBO.

Requirements of an ISO [s.1AA (6)–(7) CDA 1998]

■ Requirements included in an ISO, or directions given under such an order by a responsible officer, may require the defendant to do all or any of the following:

- Participate in activities specified in the requirements or directions at a time or times so specified
- Present her/himself to a person or persons so specified at a place or places and at a time or times so specified
- Comply with any arrangements for her/his education so specified [s.1AA(6) CDA 1998]

■ Requirements included in, or directions given under, such an order may not require the defendant to attend (whether at the same place or at different places) on more than 2 days in any 'week' (a period of 7 days beginning with a Sunday) [s.1AA (7) CDA 1998].

■ Requirements included in, and directions given under, an individual support order shall, as far as practicable, be such as to avoid any:

- Conflict with the defendant's religious beliefs and
- Interference with the times, if any, at which s/he normally works or attends school or any other educational establishment [s.1AA(8) CDA 1998]

- Before making an ISO, the court must obtain from a social worker of a local authority or a member of a YOT, and must consider, any information it considers necessary in order to determine:

  - Whether the individual support conditions are fulfilled, or
  - What requirements should be imposed by an ISO if made [s1AA(9) CDA 1998]

  NB. A 'responsible officer' in relation to an ISO means one of the following who is specified in the order: a social worker of a local authority, a person nominated by a person appointed as chief education officer under s.532 of the Education Act 1996 or a member of a YOT.

- Before making an ISO, the court must explain to the defendant in ordinary language:

  - The effect of the order and of the requirements proposed to be included in it
  - The consequences which may follow (under subsection (3)) if s/he fails to comply with any of those requirements, and
  - That the court has power (under subsection (6)) to review the order on the application either of the defendant or of the responsible officer [s.1AB(1) CDA 1998]

- If the person in respect of whom an Individual Support Order is made fails without reasonable excuse to comply with any requirement included in the order, s/he is guilty of an offence and liable on summary conviction to a fine not exceeding:

- If aged 14 or over at the date of conviction, £1,000
- If aged under 14 then, £250 [s.1AB(3) CDA 1998]

■ No referral order under s.16 (2) or (3) Powers of Criminal Courts (Sentencing) Act 2000 (referral of young offenders to youth offender panels) may be made in respect of an offence under subsection (3) above.

■ If the ASBO as a result of which an ISO was made, ceases to have effect, the ISO (if it has not previously ceased to have effect) also ceases to have effect [s.1AB (5) CDA 1998].

NB. The period specified as the term of an ISO made on an application under s.1AA(1A) must not be longer than the remaining part of the term of the ASBO as a result of which it is made [s.1AB(5A) inserted by s.124(5) CJIA 2008]

■ On an application made by complaint by the person subject to an ISO, or the responsible officer, the court which made the ISO may vary or discharge it by a further order [s.1AB (6) CDA 1998].

■ If the ASBO as a result of which an individual support order was made is varied, the court varying the ASBO may by a further order vary or discharge the ISO [s.1AB (7) CDA 1998].

Appendix 1: New Youth Justice Sentencing Structure

Pre-court: discharges & fines	YRO (requirements) as alternative to custody		Custody
Police Reprimand	Activity	Exclusion	Detention & Training Order
Final Warning	Supervision	Education	s.91 serious offence
Youth Conditional Caution	Curfew	Prohibited Activity	s.228 extended sentence/ public protection
Absolute Discharge	Programme	Electronic Monitoring	s.226 indeterminate public protection
Conditional Discharge	Residence (16/17 year olds only)	Drug Testing	s.90 mandatory life/murder
Fine	Mental Health Treatment	Drug Treatment	Intensive Supervision && Surveillance Requirement
Referral Order	Attendance Centre	LA Residence	Intensive Fostering Requirement
Reparation Order		Unpaid Work (16/17 years olds only)	
Sentence deferred		Intoxicating substance treatment	

Appendix 2: CAE Publications

From CAE Ltd Pantiles Langham Road Robertsbridge East Sussex TN32 5EP tel: 01580 880243 email: *childact@ dial.pipex.com* or order via our secure on-line facility at *www.caeuk.org*

- Children Act 1989 in The Context of Human Rights Act 1998
- Children Act 2004
- Child Protection
- Residential Care of Children
- 'How Old Do I Have To Be?'
- Sexual Offences Act 2003
- Childcare Act 2006
- Children & Young Persons Act 2008
- Safeguarding Vulnerable Groups Act 2006
- Assessment of Special Educational Needs
- ContactPoint
- Criminal Justice & Immigration Act 2008
- [forthcoming] Mental Capacity Act 2005

From CAE Scotland 105 Bishops Park Mid Calder West Lothian EH53 0SR tel: 01506 883885 email childactScotland@dsl.pipex.com

- The Children (Scotland) Act 1995 in The Context of the Human Rights Act 1998

www.caeuk.org

Discounts on orders of 50 or more of any one title